God Wants Us Back

And This Is His Plan

By

Ken C. Stratton

Photographer and Author: Ken C. Stratton

Editing and Design: Kayla Tobler

Dedicated to my lovely wife and loving family
— with love

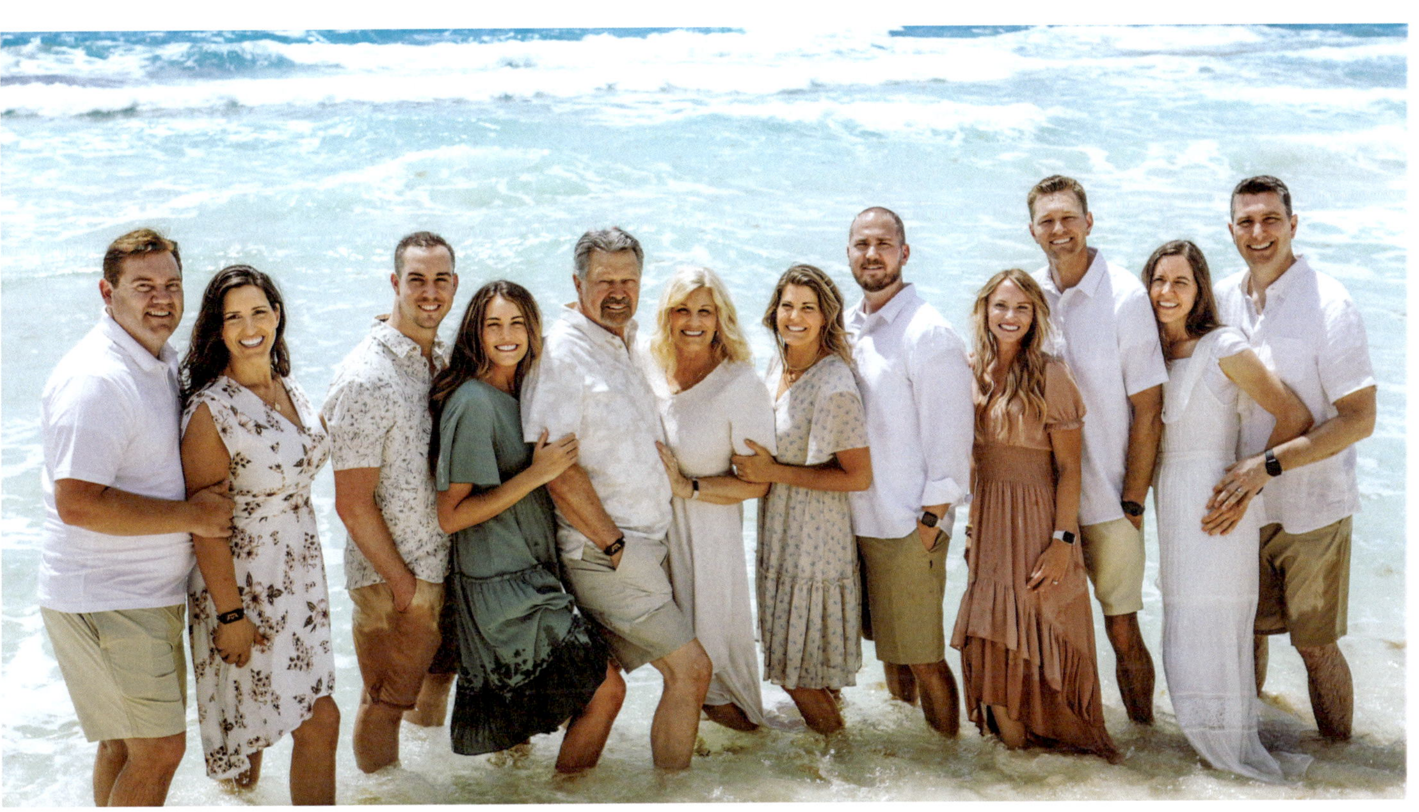

Adam * Rachel   Mike * Kayla,   Ken * Kris   Missy * Spencer   Allison * KC   Heather * Mike

VISUALIZING GOD'S PLAN THROUGH PHOTOGRAPHY

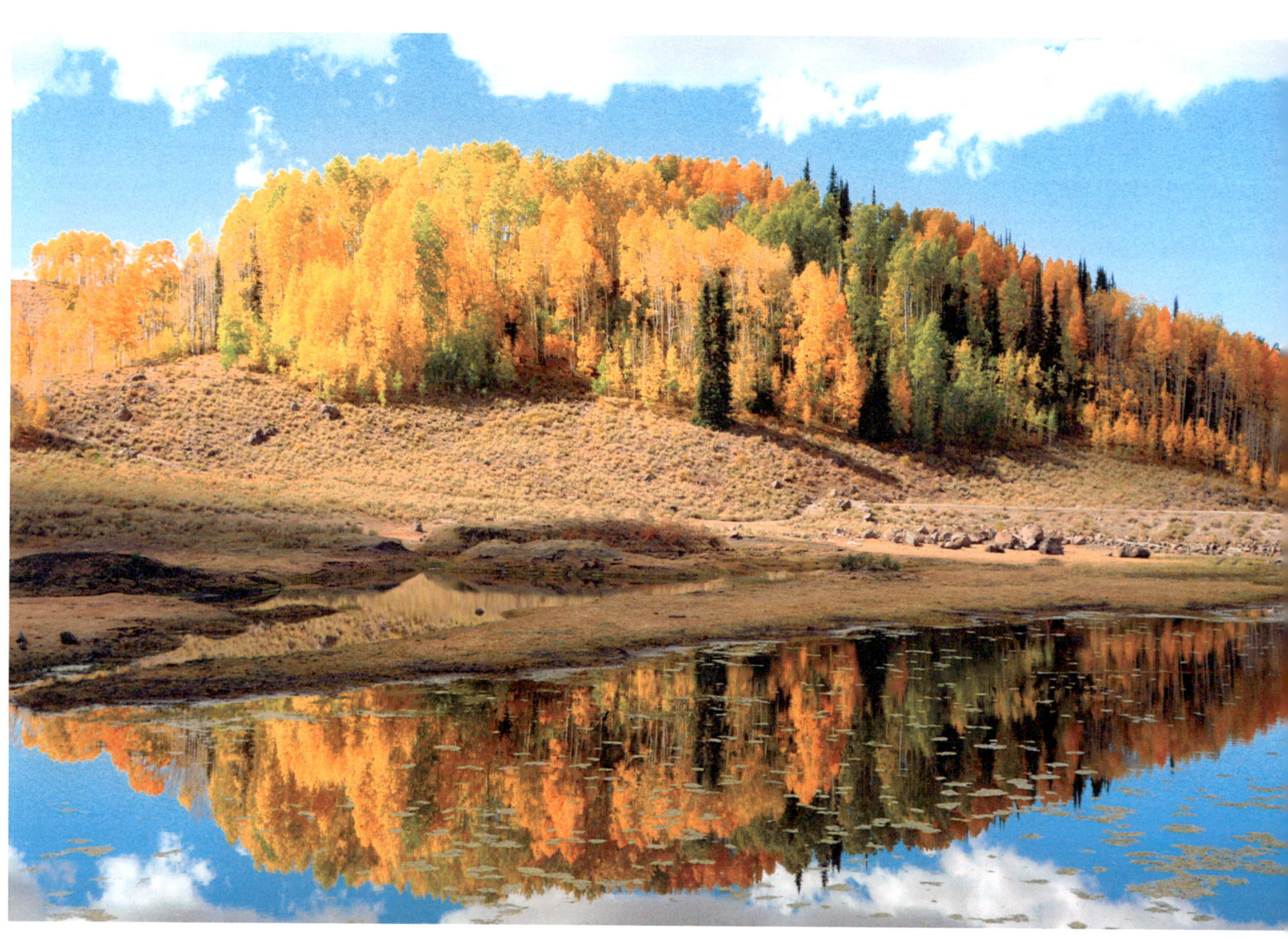

Photography has been a lifelong joy for me — a way to pause, reflect, and capture the beauty of this magnificent earth. With each photo, I've often found myself thinking not just about the scene before me, but about how it fits into something far greater: God's divine plan for us.

At the heart of that plan is this powerful truth: God wants us back. He desires every one of His children to return to Him and live with Him again. As He declares in scripture: "For behold, this is my work and my glory — to bring to pass the immortality and eternal life of man." (Moses 1:39)

As I've looked back on photos taken over the years, a thought came to me — one that shaped this book. Just like in the making of a movie, the filming happens first, and then music is added to give it meaning and emotion. In a similar way, these images represent the "filming," and the thoughts, scrip-tures, and impressions that accompany them are the "music" — together creating something deeper than either could alone.

The purpose of this book is threefold:

To introduce (or reinforce) an understanding of God's Plan for all His children — or simply to offer enjoyment through the beauty of His creations.

To emphasize the central role of Jesus Christ's Atonement, and how essential our personal acceptance of it is in the journey back to God.

To testify, through scripture and inspired words cross time, that God is unchanging – the same yesterday, today, and forever. Through photos, scrip-tures, and sacred impressions, this book is my offering – a humble expression of gratitude, faith, and hope. May it uplift, inspire, or simply invite you to see the world – and your life — through the lens of God's eternal love.

PICTURE YOURSELF STANDING ON THE BEACH AT SUNSET...

...the golden rays of the sun completely enveloping you- with what seems like the main beam of light shining only on you. Now, picture standing side-by-side next to you is your family, then your friends, the kid who once stole your bike, and even that neighborhood bully. Notice the evening sun is actually shining equally on all of you. This to me is like God's love: "It is simply always there" for everyone.   And He knows each of us by name.

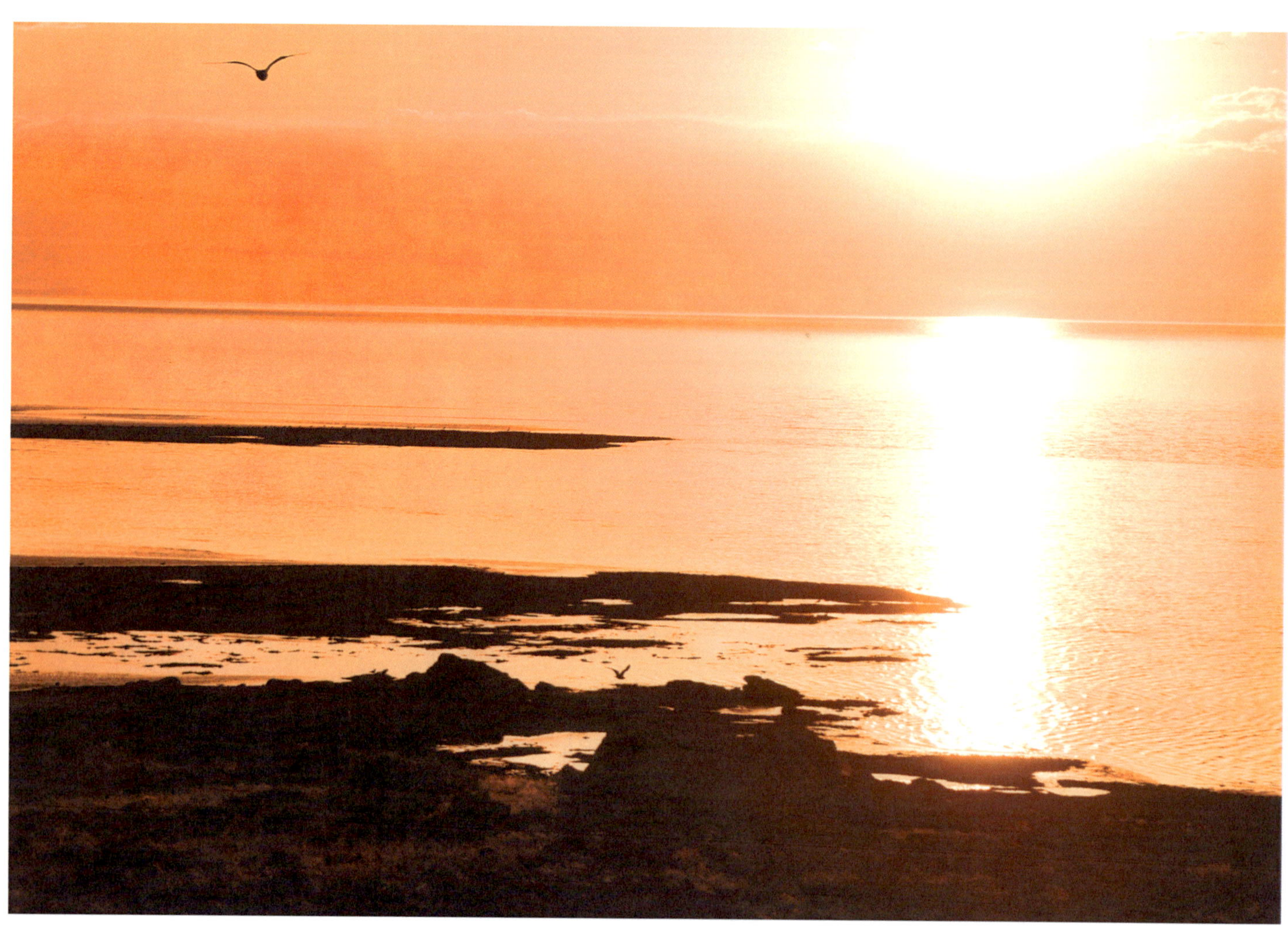

Some fairy tales begin with the phrase, "Once upon a time..." However, what follows here is not a fairy tale — it is a true account, recorded throughout history and preserved in sacred scriptures by prophets of old and reiterated and reinforced by prophets today.

And so, this begins with... "In the beginning...." (Genesis 1:1)

God, our Heavenly Father, created a vast family of spirit children in a realm often referred to as the premortal life or pre-existence. As recorded in Abraham 3:22-23: "Now the Lord had shown unto me, Abraham, the intelligences that were organized before the world was...". This doctrine is also supported by Jeremiah 1:5, where the Lord tells the prophet: "Before I formed thee in the belly I knew thee; and before thou camest forth out of the womb I sanctified thee, and I ordained thee a prophet unto the nations."

A central part of God's plan is for us to become like Him. As Jesus taught in Matthew 5:48: "Be ye therefore perfect, even as your Father which is in heaven is perfect." To become like our Heavenly Father, we needed to receive physical bodies and demonstrate our desire to return to Him by facing tests and trials on earth. The Prophet Joseph Smith explained: "We came to this earth that we might have a body and present it pure before God in the celestial kingdom. The great principle of happiness consists in having a body."

Our Heavenly Father loves us deeply. President Thomas S. Monson testified: "God's love is there for you whether or not you feel you deserve love. It is simply always there." ("We Never Walk Alone," Ensign, Nov. 2013, 124)

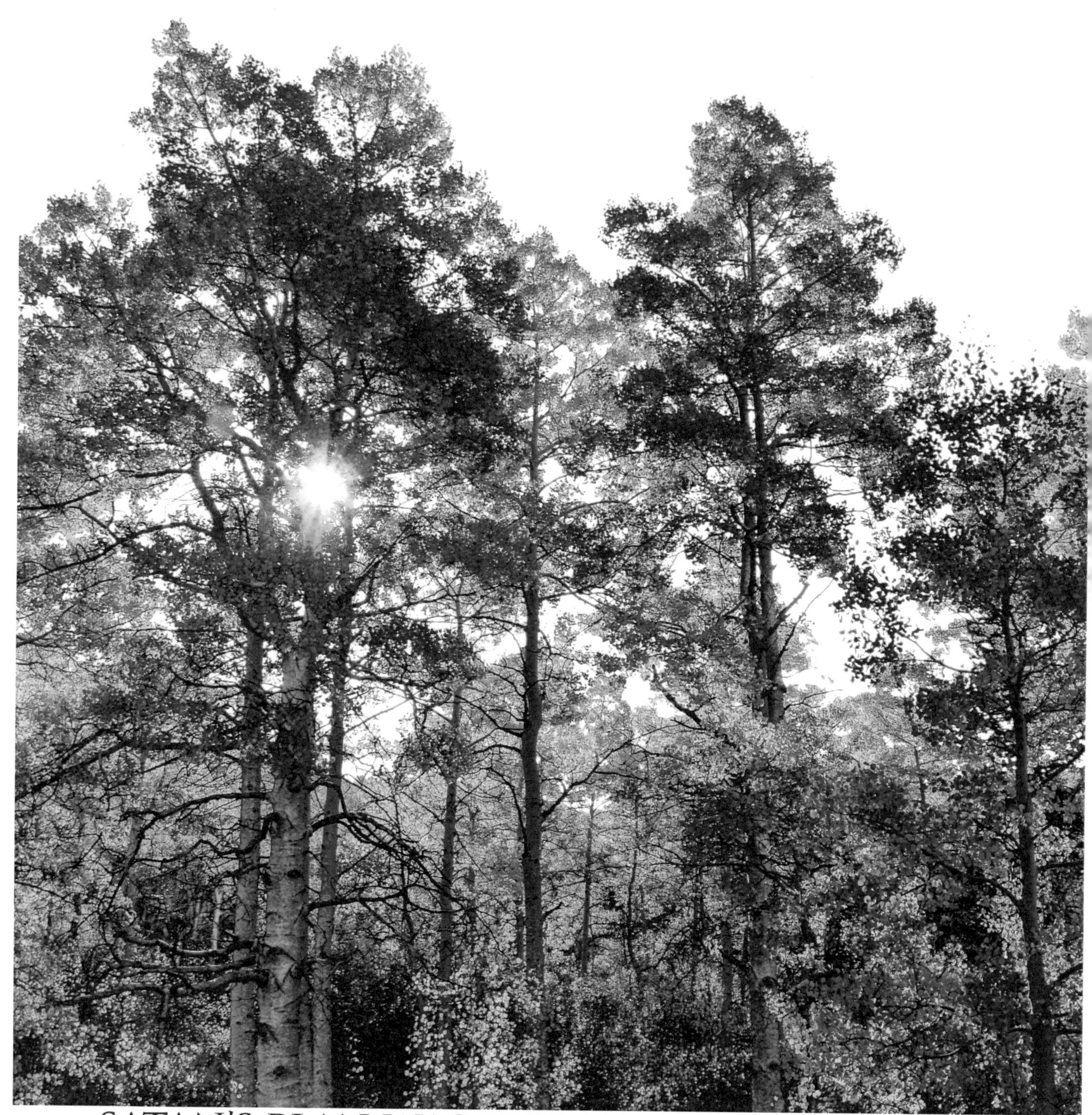

SATAN'S PLAN WAS A PLAN OF DARKNESS...

...one that would have prevented anyone from truly experiencing life. It's like walking through the world with your eyes closed, unable to see the beauty around you— missing the light of the world.

The goal of God's plan is clearly stated in Moses 1:39: "For behold, this is my work and my glory to bring to pass the immortality and eternal life of man." God's desire is for all His children to return and live with Him again. This is known as the Plan of Salvation. We are spirit children of our Heavenly Father. His "work and glory" is to help us attain immortality and eternal life. In simple terms: God wants us back.

Mortality is defined as "the state of being subject to death." We were sent to earth to receive mortal bodies in order to eventually obtain immortality, or "the ability to live forever." However, the bodies we receive in this life are not perfect. These mortal bodies are often referred to as the natural man. King Benjamin described them this way in Mosiah 3:19: "For the natural man is an enemy to God, and has been from the fall of Adam, and will be, forever and ever, unless he yields to the enticings of the Holy Spirit, and putteth off the natural man..."

That scripture highlights an essential truth: ..."unless he yields"...which implies that each of us has a choice. One of the greatest gifts Heavenly Father included in His plan is agency, or the freedom to choose. Elder Delbert L. Stapley taught: "One of God's most precious gifts to man is the principle of free agency — the privilege of choice, which was introduced by God the Eternal Father to all of His spirit children in the premortal state. This occurred in the great council in heaven before the peopling of this earth."

In that premortal council, Satan offered an alternative plan. As recorded in Moses 4:1: "...and he came before me, saying—Behold, here am I, send me, I will be thy son, and I will redeem all mankind, that one soul shall not be lost, and surely I will do it; wherefore give me thine honor." Satan's plan would have eliminated our agency. It would have prevented us from experiencing trials, growth, or the deep joy that comes from choosing righteousness. Everyone would have been saved, but not by their own will and effort.

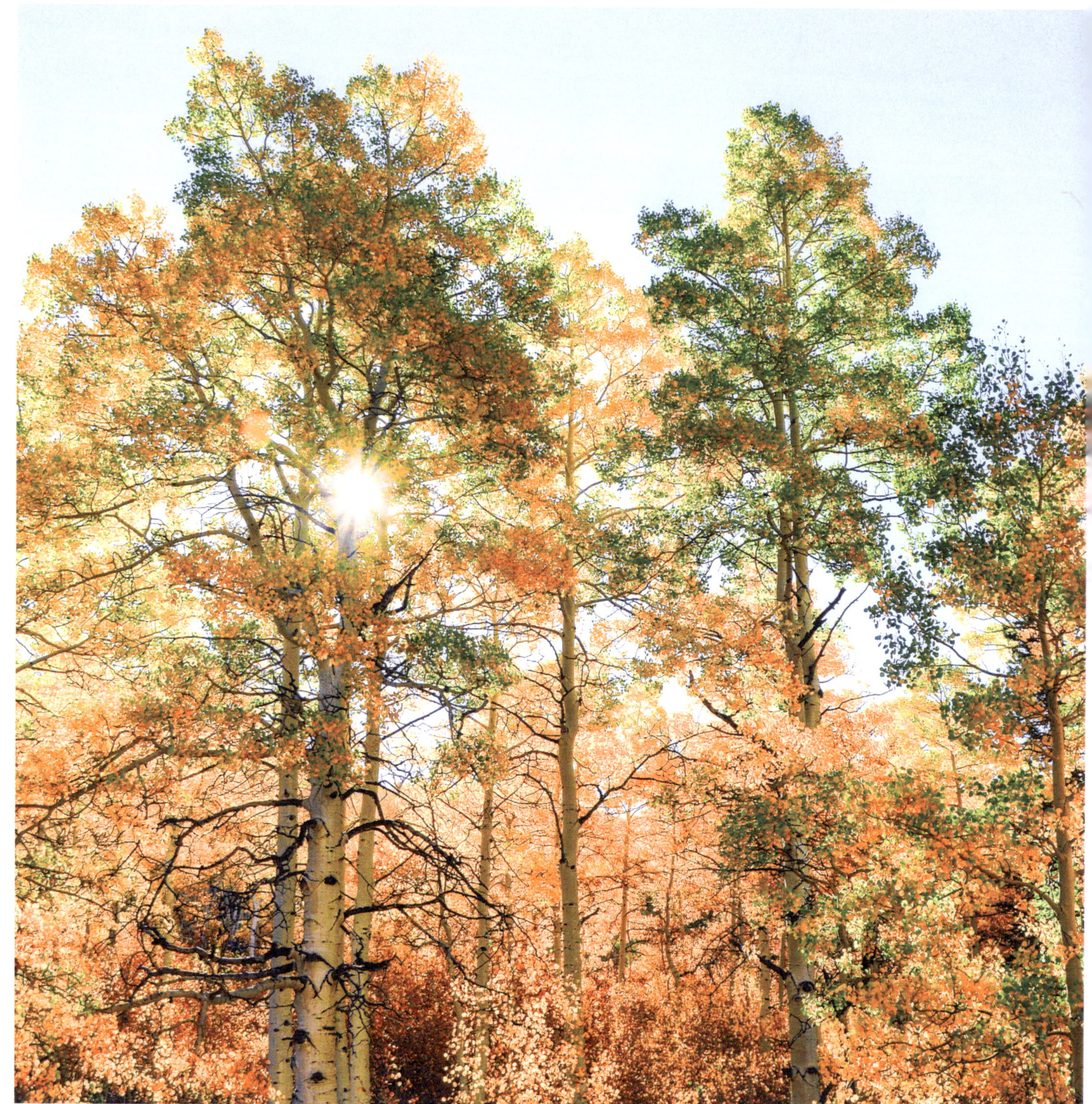

THIS PHOTO SYMBOLIZES LIFE ON EARTH...

*...which is illuminated by the Light of Christ —
revealing the beauty, detail, and richness that was hidden under Satan's
plan, as shown in the previous, identical photo. Where one leads to misery
and limitation, the other offers joy, freedom, and eternal progression.*

In the premortal council found in Moses 4:2, Heavenly Father said "...my Beloved Son, which was my Beloved and Chosen from the beginning, said unto me 'Father, thy will be done, and the glory be thine forever'." This was the plan presented by Jesus Christ.   It involved giving all of Heavenly Father's spirit children the agency to choose between right and wrong. With that agency would come the reality of sin (becoming the natural man).   But this plan also included a loving solution: a Savior, Jesus Christ, who would atone for the sins of those who chose wrong but turned to Him in faith and repentance.

The prophet Lehi, one of the   early   Nephite   prophets,   taught   the necessity of this principle in 2 Nephi 2:11:   "For it must needs be, that there is an opposition in all things.   If not so ... righteousness could not be brought to pass, neither wickedness, neither holiness nor misery, neither good nor bad."

Heavenly Father gave each of His children the divine gift of free agency. As stated in Doctrine and Covenants 29:35: "Behold, I gave unto him that he should be an agent unto himself..."   The choice we faced as spirits was to accept or reject Heavenly Father's plan presented by Jesus Christ. Regarding this time in our premortal existence, we read in D&C 38:56: "Even before they were born, they, with many others, received their first lessons in the world of spirits...". Ultimately, as taught in 2 Nephi 2:27: "Wherefore, men are free according to the flesh; ... they are free to choose liberty and eternal life, through the great Mediator of all men, or to choose captivity and death..."

CONSIDER THE DIVERSITY FOUND ACROSS THE EARTH...

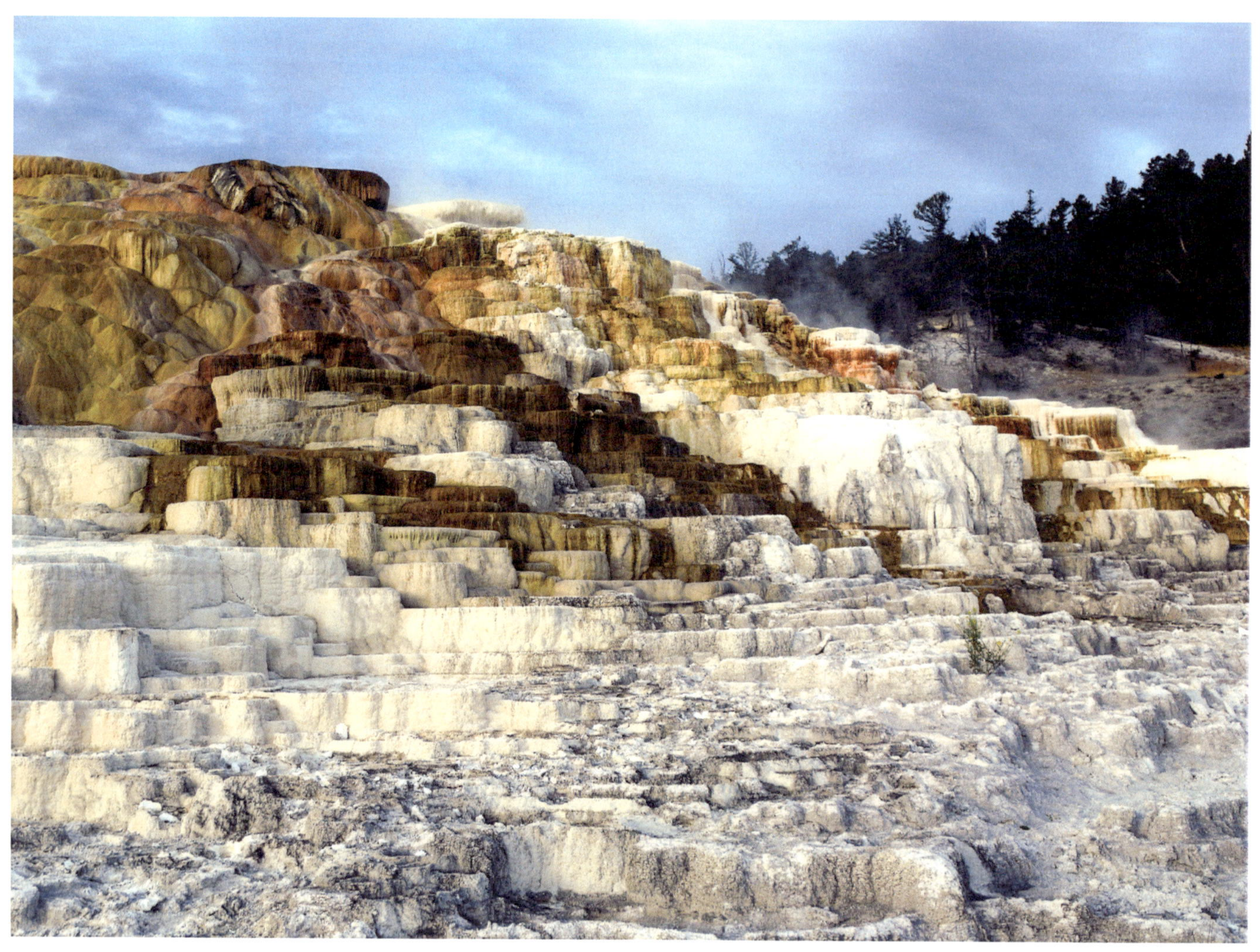

...some regions are hot, others cold; some are covered in water, others in land. In many ways, this reflects our daily lives filled with a wide range of tests and experiences. Just as the Earth was created with purpose and variety, it was also designed as a place for us to receive a body and undergo mortal testing.

Satan's attempt to alter God's divine plan led to a great war in heaven. This conflict resulted in one-third of our spiritual family being cast out of our heavenly home (the place of our spiritual birth). The Apostle John described this event in Revelation 12:7-9: "And there was war in heaven: Michael and his angels fought against the dragon; and the dragon fought and his angels, and prevailed not; neither was their place found any more in heaven. And the great dragon was cast out, that old serpent, called the Devil, and Satan, which deceiveth the whole world: he was cast out into the earth, and his angels were cast out with him."

Satan and his followers were cast out of the premortal realm and sent to earth, never allowed to receive physical bodies. Because receiving a mortal body is a necessary step to return and live with God, their eternal progression was halted. Only the few mortals who become "sons of perdition" by denying the Holy Ghost after a perfect knowledge, will be resurrected but cast into Outer Darkness having no degree of glory (D&C 76:30-38). In preparation for the rest of His children, God created the heavens and the earth for us to experience mortality and growth (Genesis 1:1).

Congratulations—you have received a physical body.

That simple fact is evidence of your choice. Though being born may seem like a basic part of life, the war in heaven reminds us it was no small matter. War implies struggle, anguish, and division — not ease or comfort. Your presence on earth means that you chose Heavenly Father's plan that Jesus Christ supported and volunteered to be the Savior. President Russell M. Nelson once said: "Grand as it is, planet Earth is part of something even grander — that great plan of God. Simply summarized, the earth was created that families might be." (General Conference, April 2000)

AS CLOUDS ARE SHAPED
BY UNSEEN FORCES...

...and governed by natural laws, and at times,
they obscure what lies beyond —
such is the veil of forgetfulness that blocks
our view of our premortal existence and
eternal truths.

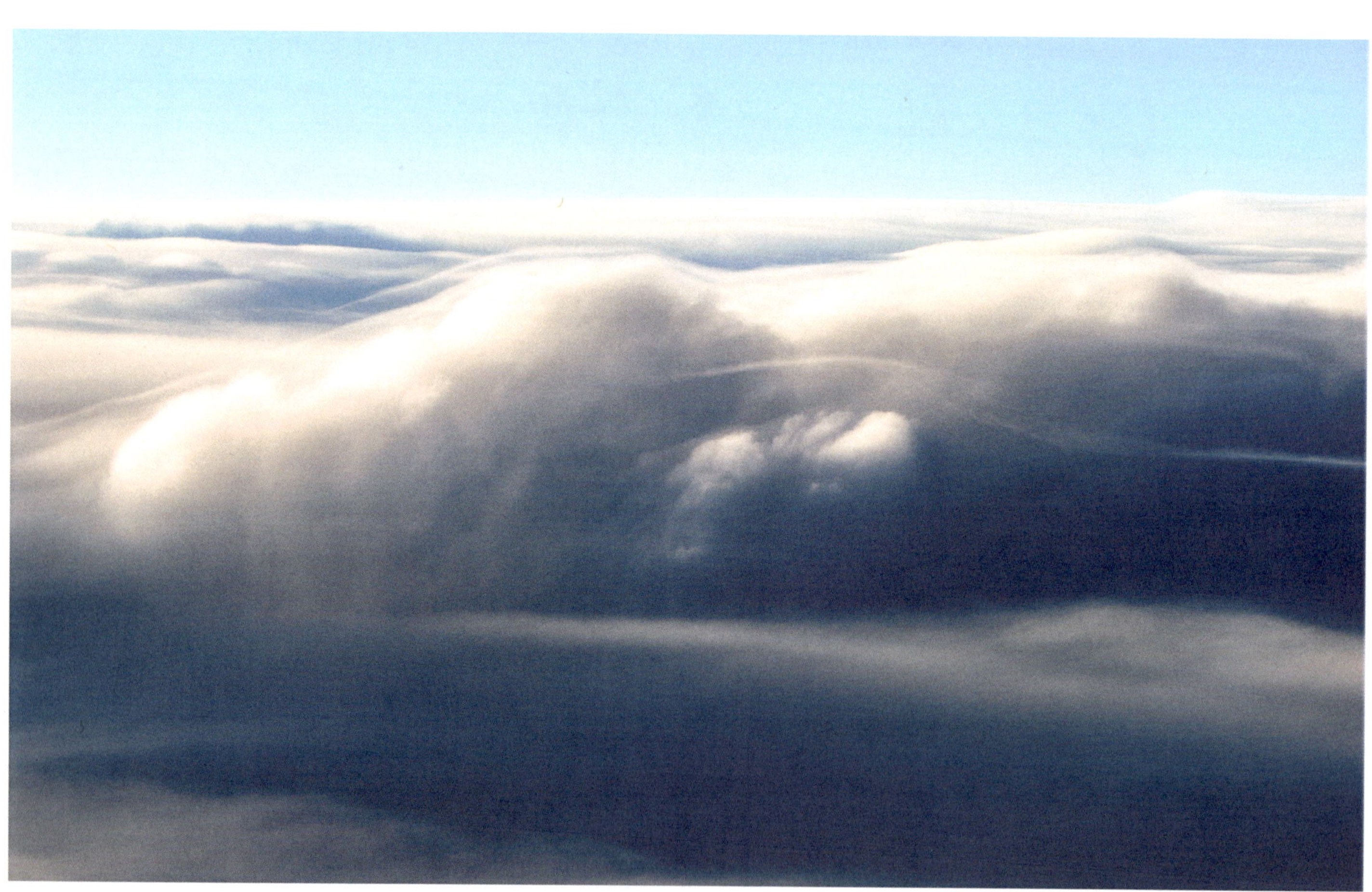

The Plan of Salvation would not truly test our faith if we remembered everything from our pre-mortal life. To ensure this test was meaningful, a veil of forgetfulness was placed over our minds. As a result, we forgot our Heavenly Parents, the choices and challenges we faced in the pre-existence, the remedy for physical and spiritual death, the path back to our Heavenly Father, and the essential requirement of accepting Jesus Christ as our Savior to fully benefit from His Atonement. Without a memory of those events, our faith is tried — we must learn to trust in what we cannot see.

The prophet Alma taught: "...The scriptures are laid before thee, yea, and all things denote there is a God; yea, even the earth, and all things that are upon the face of it, yea, and its motion, yea, and also all the planets which move in their regular form do witness that there is a Supreme Creator." (Alma 30:44)

Heavenly Father is merciful. Though we do not remember our pre-mortal life, He provides abundant evidence of His plan. He speaks through His prophets, answers prayers, performs miracles, and most importantly sent His Son to earth to serve as a perfect example, to atone for our sins, and to open the way for our resurrection. We just need to remember God's plan, Christ's Atonement, and act upon our faith.

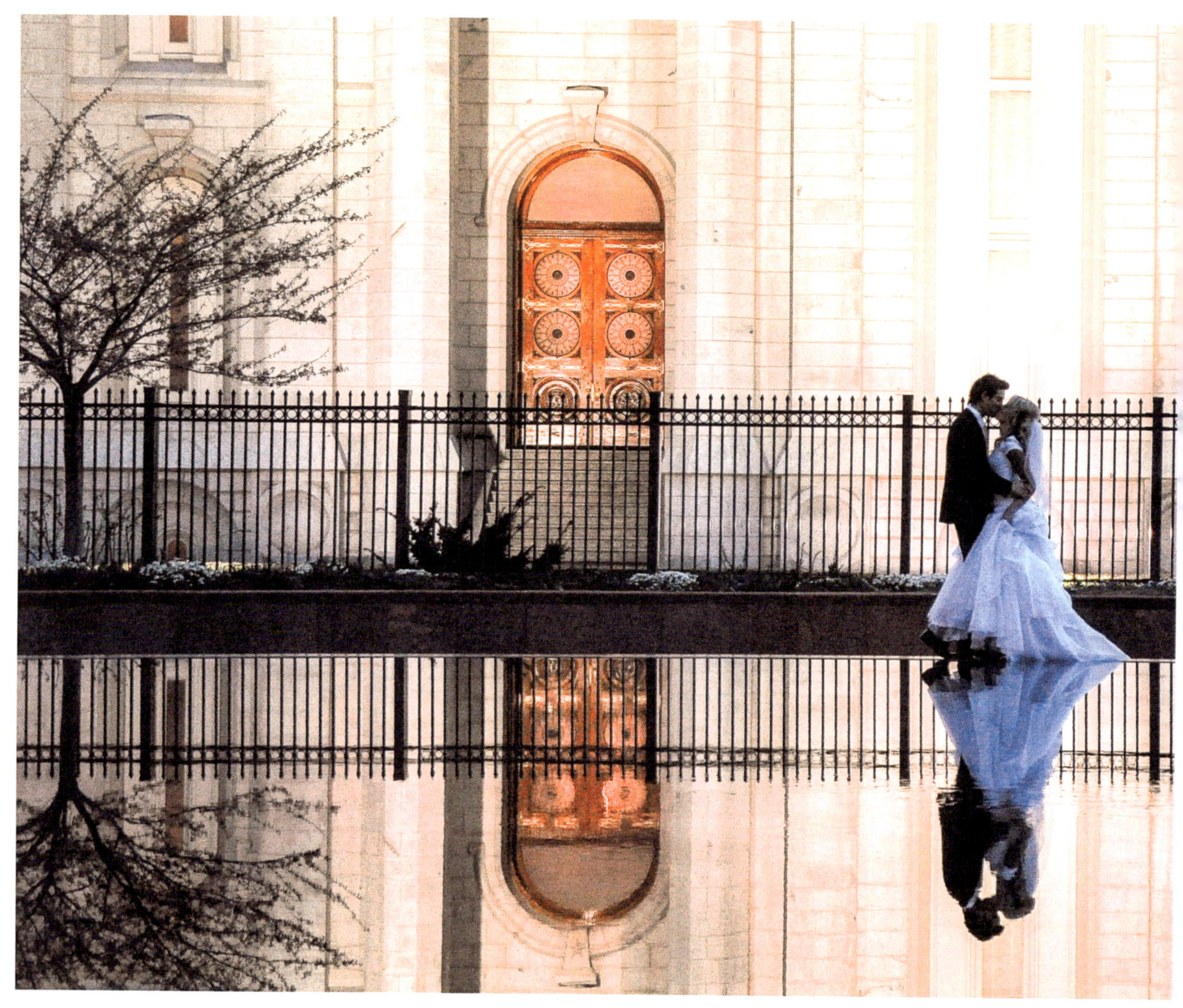

JUST AS IN MARRIAGE...

...entering into covenants with Christ is essential to fully receive the blessings of His Atonement. Belief alone is not sufficient — We must also act in faith and commitment.

The period of life on earth — sometimes called a time of happiness and misery — is a central phase in God's plan of salvation. During this mortal probation, God gave a law to Adam and Eve in the Garden of Eden: "Of every tree of the garden thou mayest freely eat: But of the tree of the knowledge of good and evil, thou shalt not eat of it." (Genesis 2:16-17) This divine command introduced agency, the ability to choose and be account-able. When Adam and Eve partook of the fruit, they broke the law, and as a result, they experienced the Fall: which is separation from God, physical death, and the introduction of sin and suffering into the world. (2 Nephi 2:22-23) This transgression was necessary for mankind to progress, yet it also marked the beginning of opposition, joy and sorrow, light and darkness, happiness and misery. (2 Nephi 2:11)

As a result of the Fall, all mankind became subject to physical death and also prone to spiritual death — separation from God through sin. The scriptures teach that "the natural man is an enemy to God" (Mosiah 3:19) and that we would be inclined toward selfishness behavior and disobedience. In this fallen state, we are incapable of returning to God on our own. Thus, a Savior was needed to bridge the gap between fallen humanity and divine justice. Jesus Christ fulfilled this need through His infinite Atonement, satisfying justice, overcoming sin and death, and offering mercy to all who would repent and follow Him. (Alma 34:9-10; John 3:16)

Elder Jeffrey R. Holland taught, "We are not only mortal beings but also spiritual beings, temporarily away from our heavenly home. Christ's sacrifice makes it possible to return." Making and keeping covenants with Heavenly Fa-ther and Jesus Christ is essential to returning to Their presence and receiving eternal life.

Covenants are sacred promises between God and His children, and they are made through priesthood ordinances such as baptism, confirmation, the sacrament, the temple endowment, and temple sealings. These covenants bind us to Christ and allow His grace to transform us as we walk the covenant path.

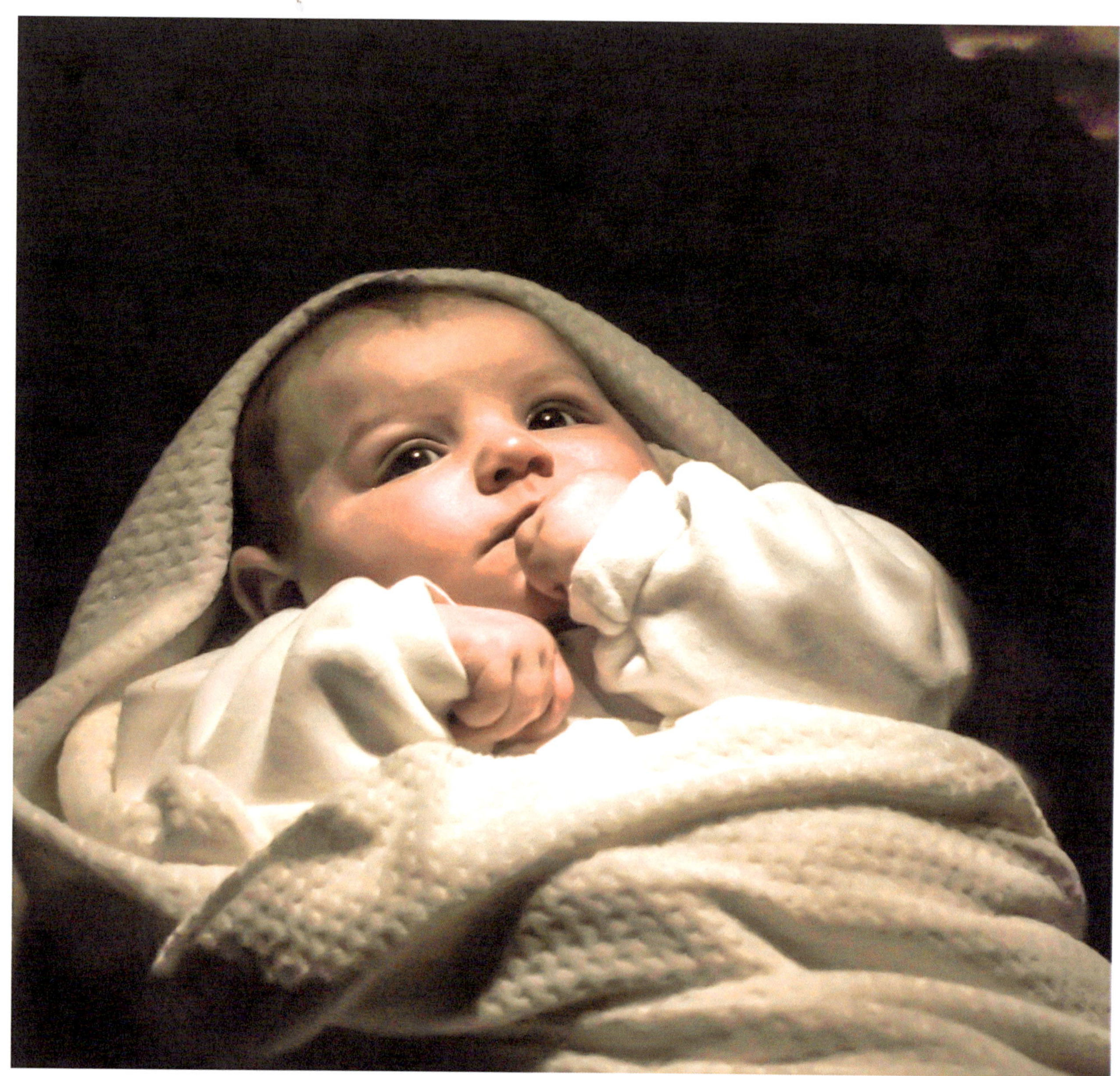

"FOR UNTO US A CHILD IS BORN, UNTO US A SON IS GIVEN…"

…as recorded in Isaiah 9:6, the Savior of the world entered quietly — yet changed everything. He came as a child, bringing the hope of eternity.

According to Alma, the next phase in God's great plan is known as the Plan of Mercy. From the very beginning, God's plan accounted for the gift of agency, granted to us in the premortal existence. With agency came the certainty that mankind would sin and fall short of divine perfection. Yet the commandment remained: "Be ye therefore perfect, even as your Father which is in heaven is perfect." (Matthew 5:48) In order to fulfill this divine expectation, a way was needed for justice to be satisfied and for mercy to be extended. That way was made possible through Jesus Christ. To fulfill His divine destiny and become like the Father, Christ Himself needed to come to earth, receive a body of flesh and bones, and experience mortality.

The Savior fully understood the immense burden that would rest upon Him — bearing the grief, pain, sorrow, and punishment for the sins of all mankind. Yet, in perfect obedience and infinite love, He willingly accepted this sacred role. Even in His suffering, He gave all glory to the Father. His life is the perfect example for us to follow. The Atonement of Jesus Christ is the central and essential part of the Plan of Salvation. Without it, there would be no way back to the presence of God. As taught in Doctrine and Covenants 18:11–12, Jesus Christ's sacrifice enables us to be saved, and His Atonement is the cornerstone upon which our hope rests. Through His Atonement, we are offered the gift of eternal life — the opportunity to return to live with our Heavenly Father.

How can we ever repay someone who made it possible for us to obtain eternal life? What offering is worthy of such a gift? The answer is simple and profound, spoken by the Savior Himself: "If ye love me, keep my commandments." (John 14:15)

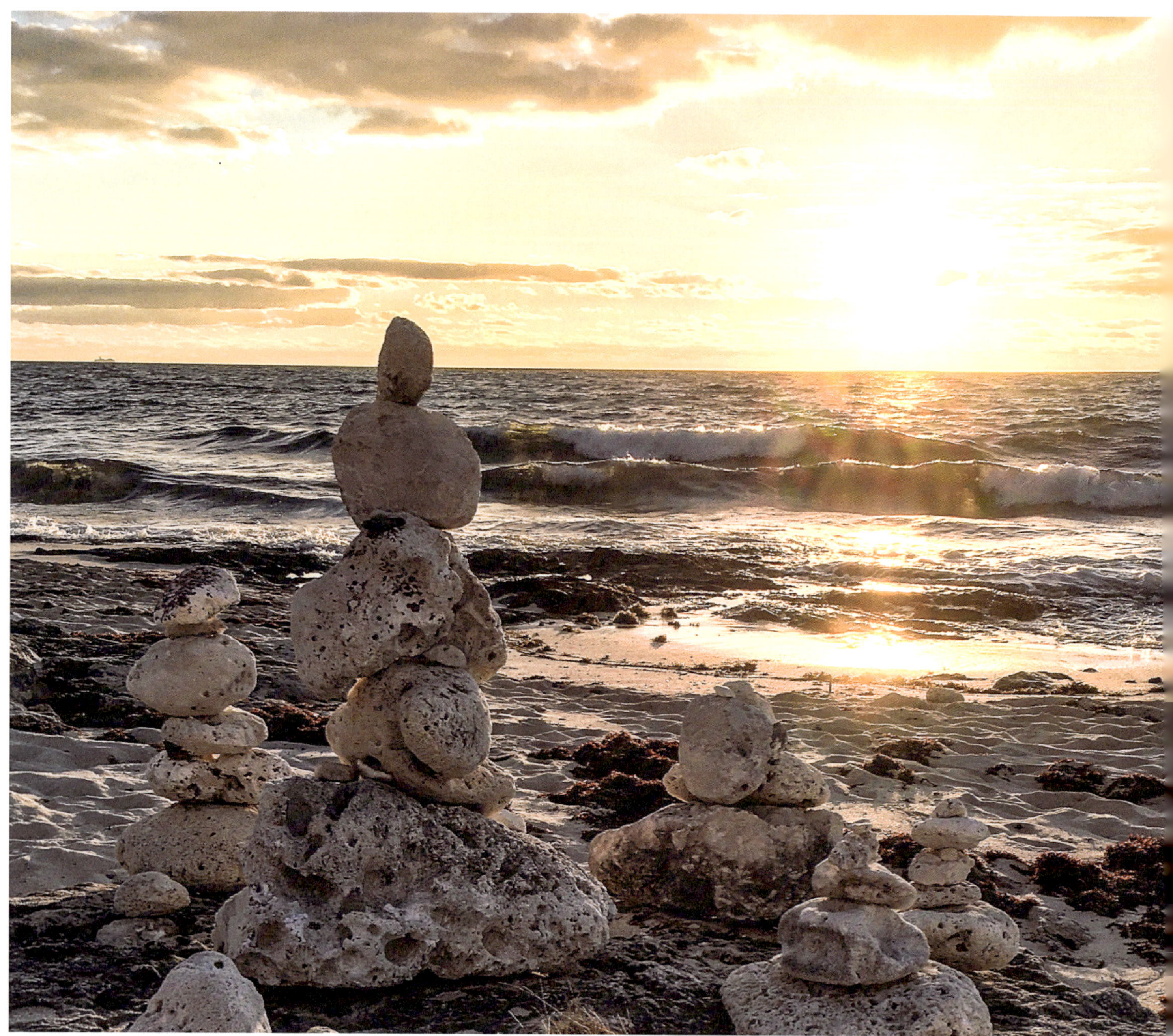

IT IS THE NATURAL MAN
WHO CONSTRUCTS THE OBSTACLES...

...that block us from fully receiving the light and love.
God's light is always present, but we often find ourselves standing
in the shadows —shadows created by our own shortcomings, doubts, and sins.

At the time of physical death, the spirit separates from the body and enters the spirit world, a temporary state before the resurrection and final judgment. The spirit world is divided into two main conditions: paradise and spirit prison. Those who lived righteously, accepted the gospel of Jesus Christ, and kept their covenants enter paradise, a state of peace, rest, and joyful anticipation of the resurrection. (Alma 40:12)

In contrast, those who rejected the gospel, lived in sin, or never had the opportunity to receive it, dwell in spirit prison — a state of learning, reflection, and, for some, suffering. (Alma 40:13-14; D&C 138:32) However, spirit prison is not a permanent punishment; it is also a place of mercy and opportunity. As revealed in Doctrine and Covenants 138, Jesus Christ organized the preaching of the gospel in the spirit world so that those in prison might accept Him, repent, and progress toward salvation.

Elder Dieter F. Uchtdorf taught, "The infinite Atonement of Christ reaches even into the spirit world, offering hope to all of God's children." This temporary division allows for continued spiritual growth and prepares each soul for resurrection and judgment. The Book of Mormon teaches that through Christ's Resurrection, all will be resurrected (Alma 11:42-44), and each will be judged according to their works. (Moroni 10:34)

THEIR TORMENT
IS AS A LAKE OF FIRE AND BRIMSTONE...

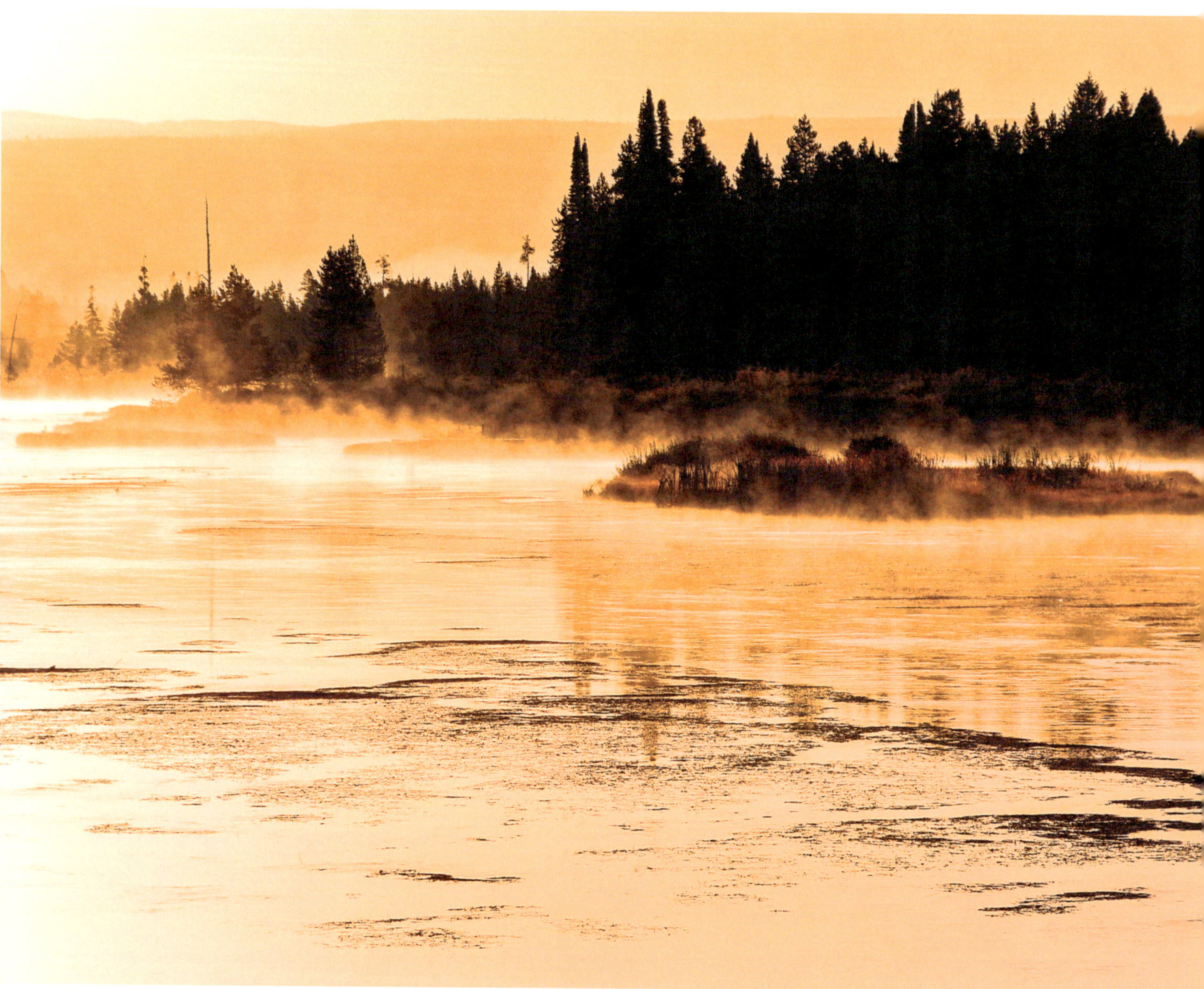

...as mentioned in Doctrine and Covenants 76, Outer Darkness is far more permanent and severe than Spirit Prison or temporal Hell. This destination is reserved for the Sons of Perdition (those who had a perfect knowledge of Christ, knew the truth fully, and chose to rebel). It is the final destination for Satan, his followers, and a very small group of mortals, and, is described as a place with no glory, complete separation from God, and eternal torment.

The Resurrection is a literal, physical, and universal event made possible through the Atonement of Jesus Christ. It is the permanent reuniting of the spirit and a perfected, immortal body, "never again to be divided." (Alma 11:43–45) This gift is given to all who have lived on the earth—both righteous and wicked — through the grace of Christ's victory over death.

President Russell M. Nelson emphasized in the April 2021 General Conference that the Resurrection is central to God's plan: "Because of Jesus Christ, all will be resurrected. This means that each of us will have the opportunity to live again, free from physical pain and death." This doctrine assures that death is not the end but a temporary separation.

Elder Dallin H. Oaks taught in April 2000 that the resurrection "will restore to every person who has lived in mortality the physical body they possessed here, renewed in its perfect form." Our resurrected bodies will be free from disease, deformity, and weakness, and will reflect the degree of glory we are worthy of — celestial, terrestrial, or telestial. (D&C 76:70, 78, 81) The Resurrection is not only a triumph over physical death, but a step toward eternal judgment and placement in God's kingdoms of glory. After this resurrection and final judgment, individuals will be assigned to one of four possible eternal destinations, each corresponding to their choices, desires, and faithfulness in mortality and the spirit world. These destinations are: the Celestial, Terrestrial, Telestial Kingdoms, and Outer Darkness.

Outer Darkness, the fourth and most severe destination, is reserved for the "sons of perdition" — those who had a perfect knowledge of Christ and then willfully denied Him and fought against God. (D&C 76:31–38) These are few in number, and their fate is spiritual exile, where "their torment is as a lake of fire and brimstone." (D&C 76:36)

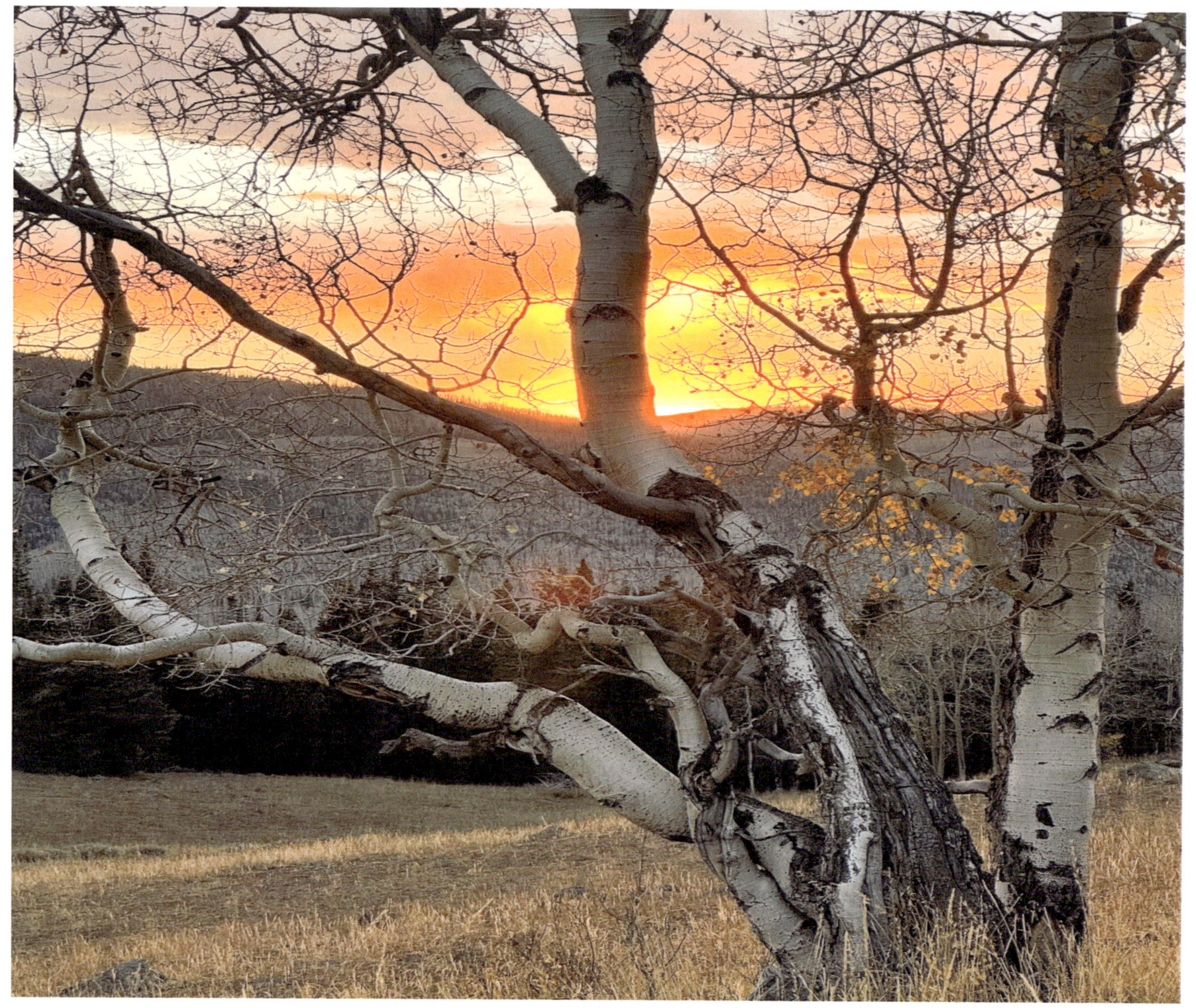

LIFE'S TEMPTATIONS, SHORTCOMINGS, AND SINS COULD LEAVE NOTICEABLE SCARS...

...as characterized in this photo of the tree. By not applying the principle of repentance and accepting Christ as the Savior, those sins are not washed away.   This leaves the soul "unclean". Alma 40:26 "...the wicked remain as though there had been noredemption made, except it be the loosing of the bands of death; for behold, the day cometh that all shall rise from the dead and stand before God, and be judged according to their works." Moses 6:57 "...no unclean thing can dwell there, or dwell in his presence."

John 14:2 Jesus tell us that there is more to the afterlife than just heaven and hell: "In my Father's house are many mansions: if it were not so, I would have told you. I go to prepare a place for you."

In 1 Corinthians 15:41 it states: "There is one glory of the sun, and another glory of the moon, and another glory of the stars: for one star differeth from another star in glory." Compared to the sun or moon, the Telestial Kingdom is just a small twinkle in the sky.

The Telestial Kingdom is the lowest of the three degrees of glory in the afterlife, yet it is still a kingdom of immense beauty and glory. Those who inherit the Telestial glory are individuals who did not receive the gospel of Jesus Christ or accept His testimony in mortality or in the spirit world, and who were not valiant in their testimony. (Doctrine and Covenants 76:81–82, 102–103) They include liars, sorcerers, adulterers, and others who continued in their sins and refused to repent. (D&C 76:103)

And in Mosiah 15:26 it informs us that those destined for this kingdom have no part in the first resurrrection. These individuals suffer in spirit prison until the end of the Millennium, after which they are resurrected and assigned to this kingdom. Though they do not receive the presence of the Father or the Son, they are visited by the Holy Ghost and are ministered to by angels. (D&C 76:86–88)

Despite being the lowest kingdom, its glory "surpasses all understanding" (D&C 76:89), highlighting the mercy and justice of God in providing a degree of eternal happiness even for the least obedient.

HERE THE AIR IS CRISP WITH THE SURROUNDING
QUIET MAJESTY OF NATURE. BUT ABOVE
YOU, CLOUDS HANG LOW, MUTING OUT THE
BRILLIANCE OF THE SUN.

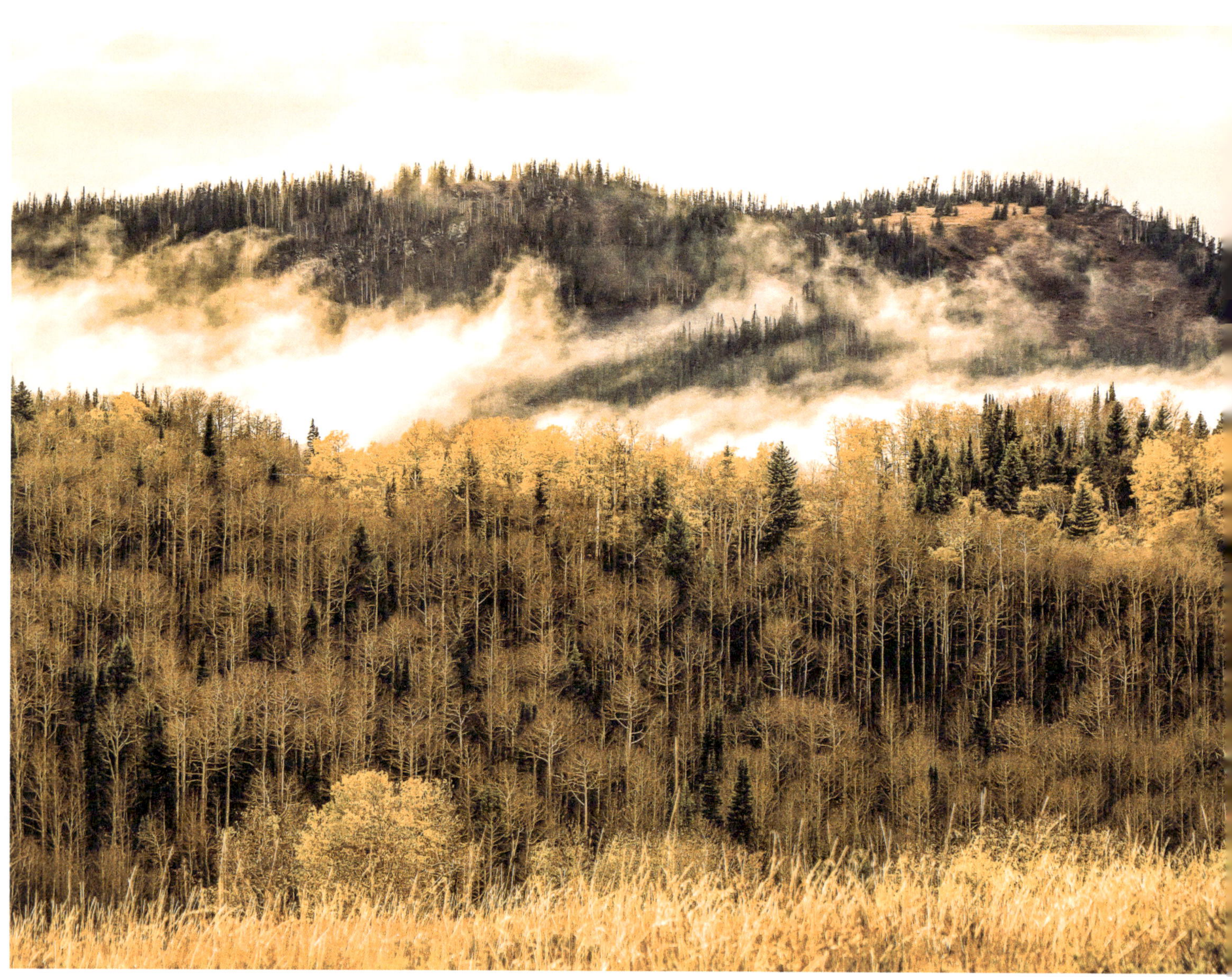

*Imagine standing on this high ridge. The landscape is breathtaking—
vibrant golds and oranges blanket the hillsides. While this scene is
beautiful, it's not bathed in full light. The peaks stretch higher still—
beyond the clouds—where the sun shines unobstructed. Hence, those that
obtain this glory enjoy its beauty, but it's not the Celestial Kingdom. And,
more importantly, they do not dwell with Heavenly Father.*

The Terrestrial Kingdom is the middle degree of glory in the afterlife. It is a kingdom of great beauty and peace, reserved for honorable individuals who were not valiant in their testimony of Jesus Christ. According to Doctrine and Covenants 76:71–79, this includes those who were "honorable men of the earth" who were blinded by the natural man, as well as those who did not accept the gospel in mortality but did receive it in the spirit world. It also includes members of the Church who were not valiant in their discipleship. Though they receive the presence of Jesus Christ, they do not receive the fullness of the Father. (D&C 76:77) They are not partakers of the celestial glory, yet their reward is still glorious beyond mortal comprehension.

Elder Dallin H. Oaks, in his April 2011 General Conference talk, emphasized the eternal importance of choices made in mortality: "In the Final Judgment we will stand before the Savior, not only to be judged for our acts, but also to receive the reward that we have merited." The Terrestrial Kingdom is a reflection of that principle — it is a reward for those who lived good lives, but who did not fully embrace the covenant path.

As we see in the description of God's kingdoms - that obedience to His laws are critical. We were offered and we accepted free agency in the pre-mortal life. Yet, our beings having 'natural man' tendencies, it seems like the most difficult thing to do is obey God's law.

President Russell M. Nelson has also repeatedly taught that exaltation requires intentional discipleship and covenant keeping, indicating that the Terrestrial Kingdom, while glorious, is not the destination for those who seek eternal progression with God. The Lord's plan is merciful and just, offering a place for all His children, each according to their faith, repentance, and choices. (2 Nephi 2:27–29)

OUR ULTIMATE AND ETERNAL GOAL...

*...to return to the presence of God and dwell in the
Celestial Kingdom, where we can live in everlasting joy
with our Heavenly Father and our families.*

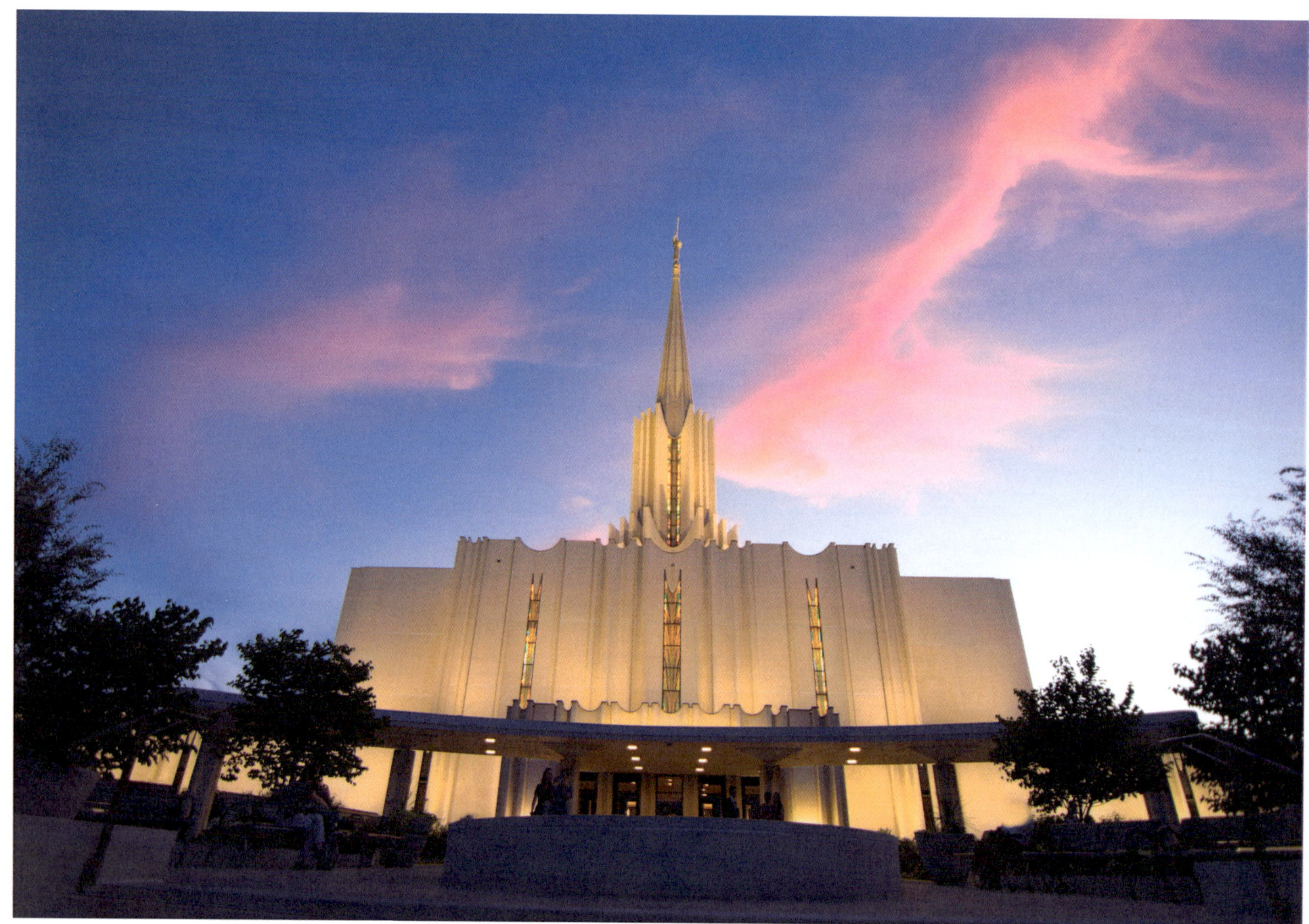

It's natural to see someone treat a gift with less care when it's freely given. But notice the difference when that same person must work diligently, directly, and with determination to earn it — the gift is valued and respected far more deeply.

It's often said, "To whom much is given, much is expected." But consider this as well: "To where much is devoted, reverenced, and pursued with a heart striving for perfection — much is given."

The Celestial Kingdom is the highest glory, reserved for those who have accepted Jesus Christ, repented of their sins, received saving ordinances, and endured faithfully to the end. (Doctrine and Covenants 76:50-70)

To obtain the Celestial Kingdom, we must:

Have accepted and followed Christ in the premortal existence

Come to earth, receive a body, and demonstrate our willingness to live by God's commandments

Make and honor baptismal and temple covenants

Acknowledge Jesus Christ as the Savior and Redeemer of the world

Fully embrace and apply the blessings of His Atonement

Be resurrected — our spirit and body reunited through God's mercy

Be judged according to our thoughts, words, and actions

And ultimately, choose and desire to live eternally in the presence of God and Jesus Christ

"Celestial kingdom... is life eternal in the presence of our Father in Heaven. It is the greatest gift of God. In the celestial kingdom, we receive "of his fulness, and of his glory." Indeed, all that the Father hath shall be given unto us."   President Dieter F. Uchtdorf (October Confernce 2015)

WE MAY NOT SEE HIS FOOTSTEPS IN THE SAND NEXT TO OURS...

...nor see Him walking beside us on this journey toward eternal life.
But, if we are doing what is right and giving our all,
we will feel His presence.

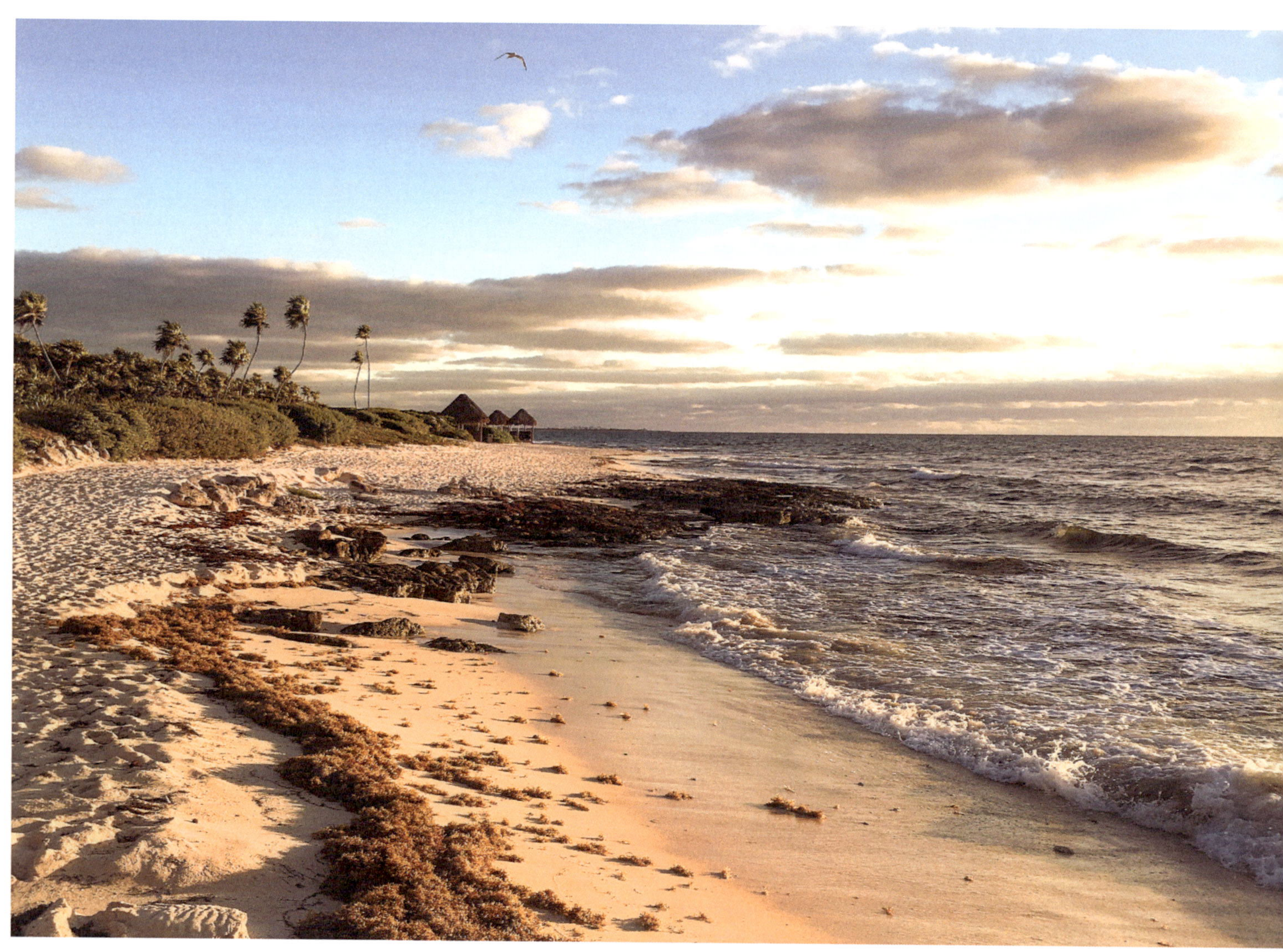

> *"Wherefore, be of good cheer,*
> *and do not fear,*
> *for I the Lord am with you,*
> *and will stand by you."*
>
> Doctrine and Covenants 68:6

What a powerful reassurance! These words are a reminder that no matter the trials, uncertainties, or opposition we face, we are never alone. The Lord's promise is not conditional on perfection, but on our faith and willingness to follow Him.

When we feel overwhelmed by life's burdens or discouraged by our weaknesses, this verse invites us to move forward with courage, knowing that the Savior walks beside us. His presence gives strength beyond our own and hope beyond the moment. It is a call to trust that He is near and to find peace in His unwavering support.

A LIGHTHOUSE CASTS LIGHT TO GUIDE US THROUGH DARKNESS AND DANGER

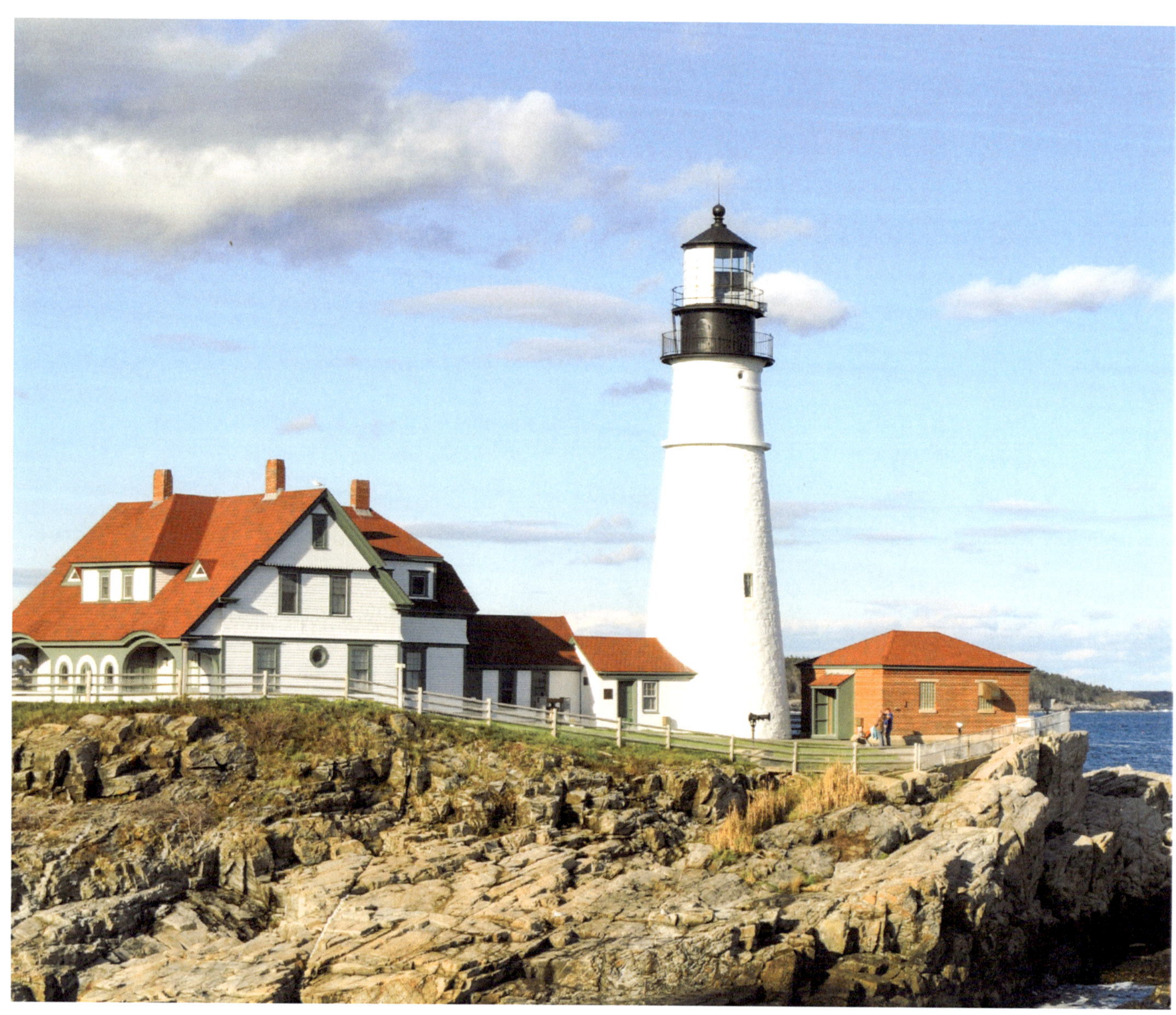

*Similarly, a prophet also points the way to safe passage
and the Celestial Kingdom. To think celestial is to shift
our short-range focus from the temporary concerns of this
life to the eternal perspective of God's plan.*

Think Celestial: President Nelson's talk (October 2023 General Conference) reminds us that our journey here on earth defines our eternal destiny. It will determine: where we will live eternally; the condition of our resurrected bodies; and, with whom we will dwell with forever.

What does it really mean to "Think Celestial"? Simply stated: "Put Jesus Christ first."

Key components of President Nelson's talk:

- Adopt an eternal mindset: Pause and ask, "What would a celestial perspective guide me to do?"
- Daily alignment with celestial principles: Incorporate prayer, scripture study, temple worship, repentance, and faithful living to train your mind and heart.
- Apply gospel principles in real life: Choose actions that align with eternity while facing trials, choosing entertainment, and managing disappointment.
- Eternal outcomes matter: Remember, our choices now have lifelong and eternal implications — on our joy, relationships, and to which kingdom we will be resurrected.

THE HOUR HAS COME

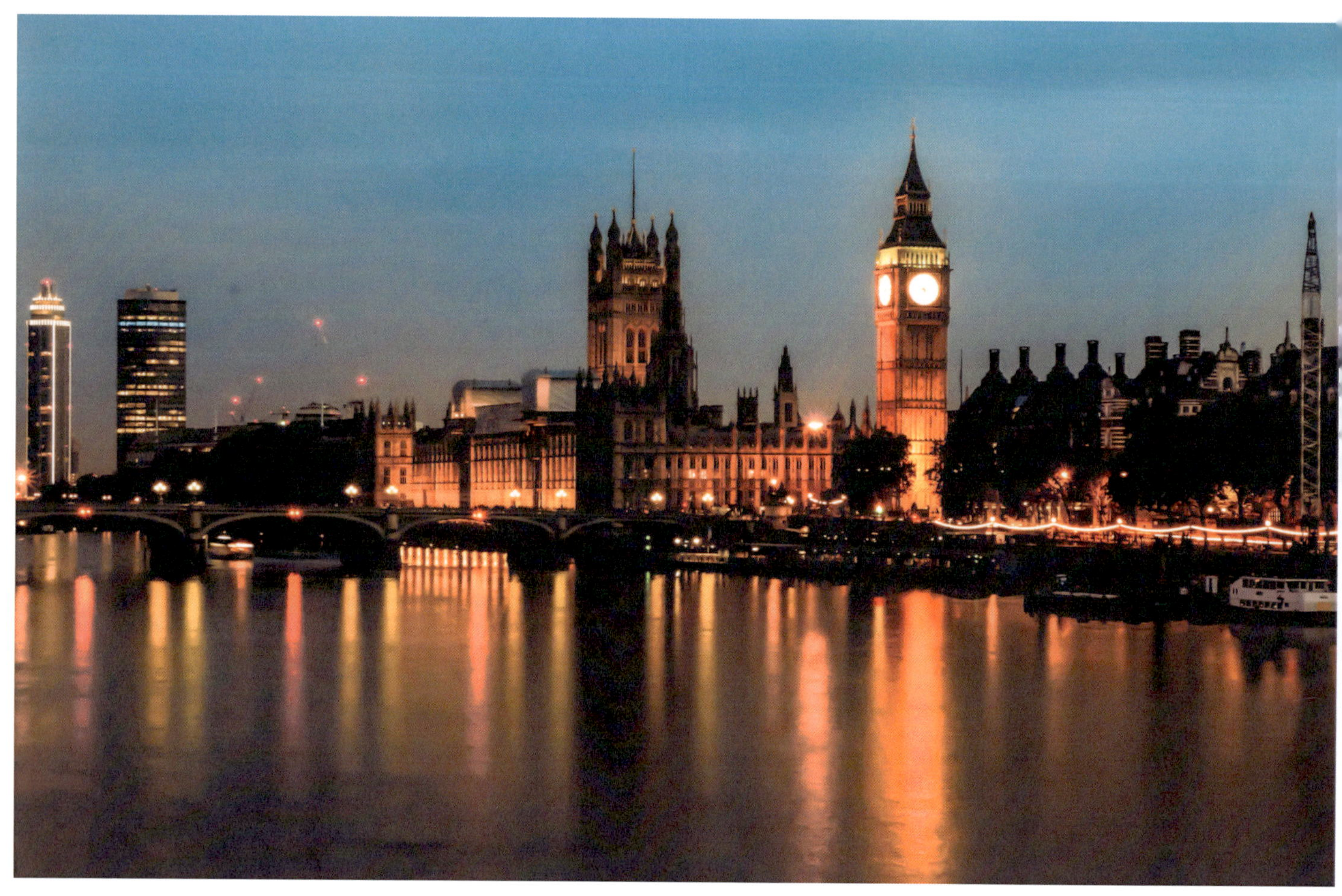

D&C 14:7 *"For behold, this life is the time for men to prepare to meet God; yea, behold the day of this life is the day for men to perform their labors.*

APPENDICES

Plans and Laws to return to Him

Scriptural Summary

Referenced scriptural books, other content and their timelines

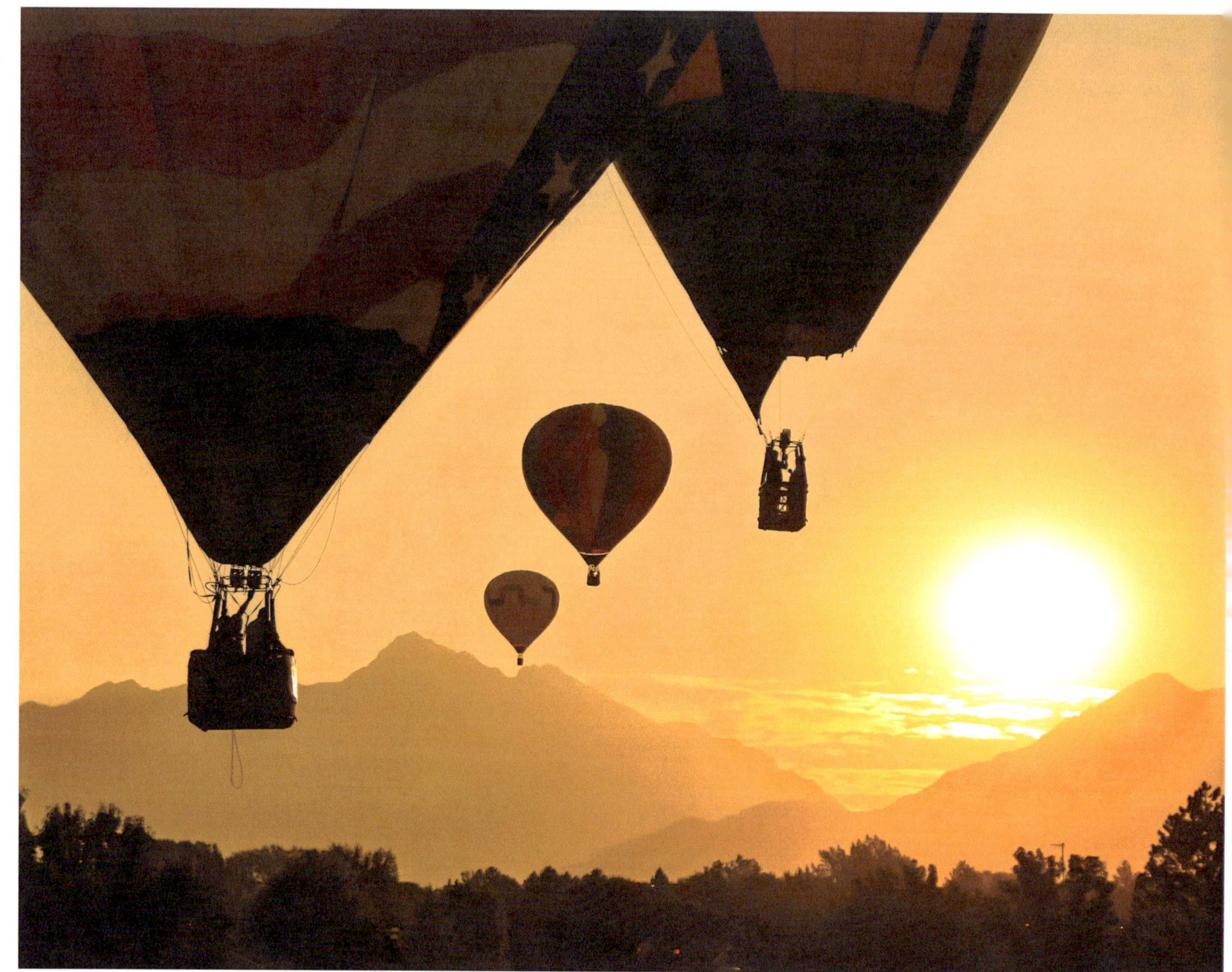

PLANS AND LAWS
TO RETURN TO HIM

God's plan—

> *from the pre-existence,*
> *to the earth and mortal creation,*
> *through the Fall,*
> *the Atonement,*
> *the Resurrection,*
> *and Judgement*

— provides a way back to Him.

I. Our Spiritual Beginning / Premortal Plan

Man's Spirit Created and Sent to Earth

Doctrine: We are spirit children of our Heavenly Father, created in the premortal life.

Scripture: Jeremiah 1:5 –

"Before I formed thee in the belly I knew thee..."

Key Point: We chose to follow Christ's plan in the premortal council and were given the opportunity to come to earth to receive a body and be tested.

II. The Law Was Given

Event: In the Garden of Eden, God gave Adam and Eve a commandment — not to eat the fruit of the tree of knowledge of good and evil.

Scripture: Genesis 2:17 – "For in the day that thou eatest thereof thou shalt surely die."

Key Point: God gave agency and a law — obedience would lead to eternal life; disobedience would bring consequences.

III. The Law Was Broken – The Fall of Adam

Doctrine: Adam and Eve partook of the fruit, bringing the Fall.

Result: Two types of death entered:

Temporal Death: Separation of body and spirit.

Spiritual Death: Separation from God's presence.

Scripture: 2 Nephi 2:25 – "Adam fell that men might be; and men are, that they might have joy."

IV. The Plan of Happiness and Misery

Concept: The Fall made us subject to both joy and sorrow. Earth life would include opposition.

Scripture: 2 Nephi 2:11 – "It must needs be, that there is an opposition in all things..."

Key Point: Life on earth provides a chance to experience growth, joy, trials, and the ability to choose (free agency).

V. The Plan to Overcome Spiritual Death

Doctrine: Though the Fall created spiritual death, Christ's mission was to overcome it.

Scripture: Alma 42:9 - "The soul could never die, and the fall had brought upon all mankind's spiritual death..."

Key Point: God provided a Savior to redeem us from the effects of the Fall.

VI. Christ's Death and Resurrection - The Plan of Mercy

Doctrine: Christ overcame both physical and spiritual death through His Atonement and Resurrection.

Scripture: Mosiah 16:7-8 - "...there is a resurrection, therefore the grave hath no victory, and the sting of death is swallowed up in Christ.

Key Point: This gift is available to all mankind through grace and individual choice.

VII. The Atonement and the Law of Justice

Doctrine: Since the law was broken, justice demanded consequence. Christ satisfied that justice through His Atonement.

Scripture: Alma 34:16 - ""And thus mercy can satisfy the demands of justice..."

Key Point: Through Christ, justice is fulfilled and mercy is extended to all who repent.

VIII. Redemption and Eternal Destiny - The Plan of Salvation

Doctrine: If we accept Christ and live His gospel, we may be redeemed and inherit eternal life.

Scripture: Doctrine and Covenants 76 - Describes the degrees of glory: Celestial, Terrestria, Telestial.

Key Point: Our actions and acceptance of Christ determine our spiritual destination.

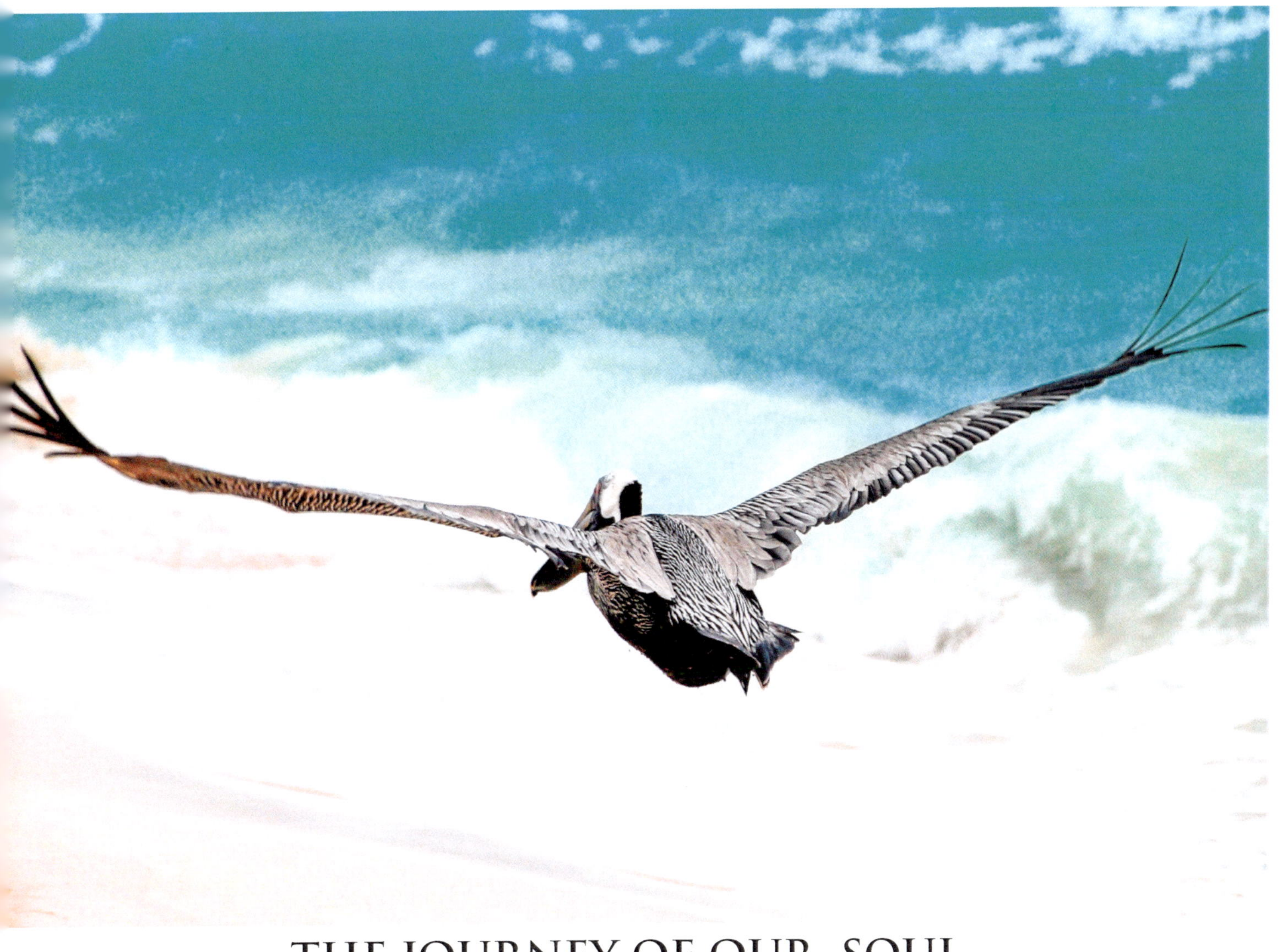

THE JOURNEY OF OUR SOUL

From spirit creation, to mortality, to resurrection is made meaningful and purposeful through God's eternal plan.

The Fall made salvation necessary, and Christ made salvation possible.

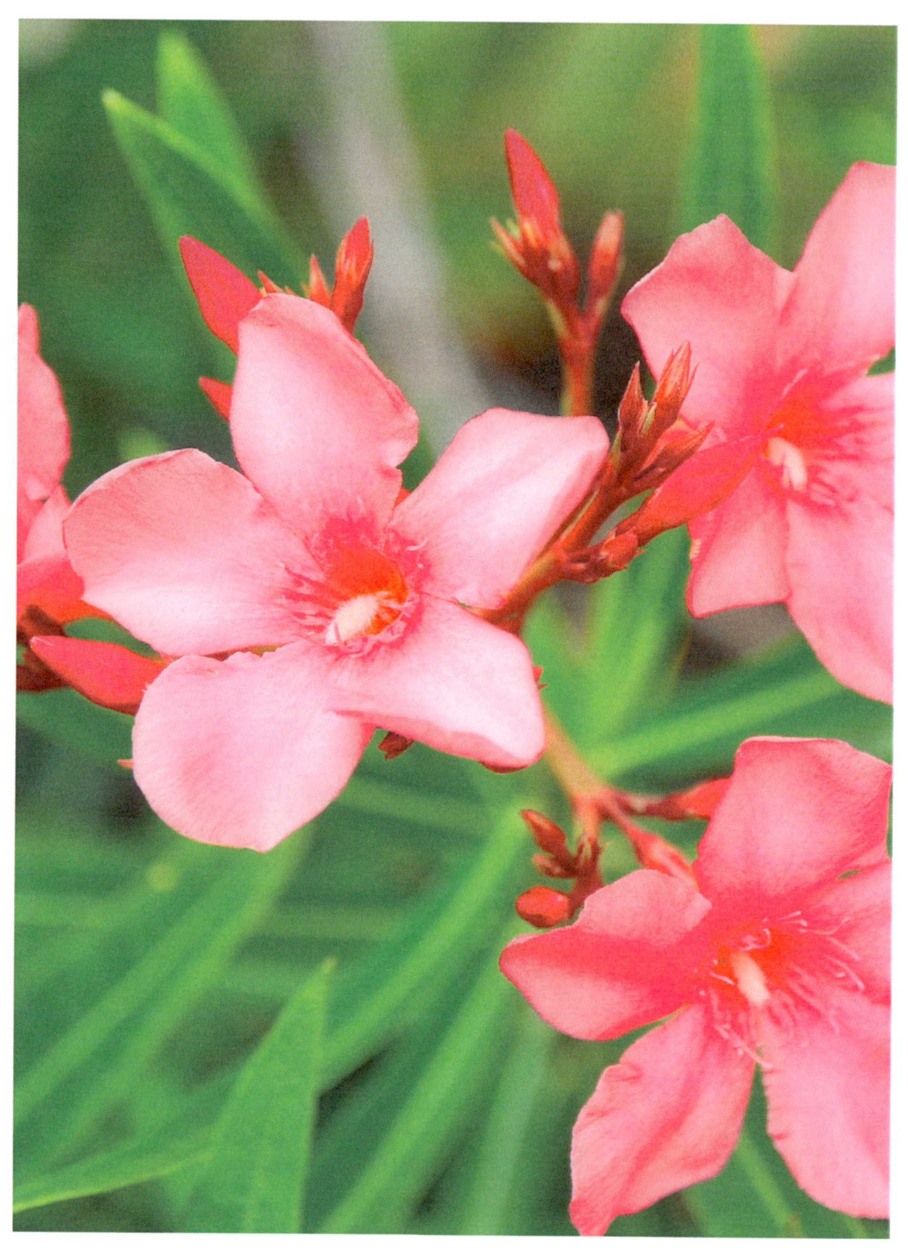

SCRIPTURAL SUMMARY

The Plan of Salvation describes God's purpose for His children, the path to return to His presence, and the role of

Jesus Christ in that process.

I. Premortal Life

Holy Bible: The Bible references the premortal existence in Jeremiah 1:5, where God knew the prophet before he was born.

Book of Mormon: Teaches that all people lived with God before coming to earth (Abraham 3:22-23, Alma 13:3).

Doctrine and Covenants: In D&C 93:29, it reveals that all spirit children existed with God before coming to earth.

II. Creation

Holy Bible: Genesis 1:1 states that God created the heavens and the earth, preparing a place for His children.

Pearl of Great Price: The Book of Abraham elaborates on the creation of the world and the organization of the earth.

III. The Fall of Adam and Eve / Plan of Happiness and Misery

Holy Bible: The Fall in Genesis 3 explains how Adam and Eve's transgression introduced mortality and the need for redemption.

Book of Mormon: Lehi teaches in 2 Nephi 2:25 that Adam's fall was necessary for us to have the opportunity to grow, learn, and progress.

Doctrine and Covenants: D&C 29:40-46 explains that with man's free agency, the fall brought sin, and the need for a Savior.

IV. Earthly Life and Agency

Holy Bible: The Bible demonstrates agency, as seen in passages like Joshua 24:15 ("Choose you this day whom ye will serve").

Book of Mormon: Agency is a fundamental teaching. In 2 Nephi 2:27, it explains that all men are free to choose liberty and eternal life through Jesus Christ or choose captivity and death.

Doctrine and Covenants: D&C 58:26-29 reinforces the concept of free will, stating that we are accountable for our choices.

V. Atonement of Jesus Christ / Plan of Mercy

Holy Bible: The Atonement is essential, as written in John 3:16, where it speaks of Christ's sacrifice for the salvation of mankind.

Book of Mormon: Christ's Atonement is emphasized, especially in Alma 34:8-7, where it explains how Jesus Christ's suffering and death atoned for sins and made the resurrection possible. It also teaches that through the Atonement of Christ, one can gain eternal life and return to God's presence (Mormon 9:14).

Pearl of Great Price: The Book of Moses and Abraham also mention Christ's central role in the creation and redemption of mankind (Moses 4:1-4, Abraham 3:27-28).

Doctrine and Covenants: D&C 18:11-12 teaches that Jesus Christ's sacrifice enables us to be saved and that His Atonement is the cornerstone of the Plan of Salvation.

VI. Death, Resurrection, and Judgment

Holy Bible: The resurrection and judgment are essential doctrines in the Bible, as in 1 Corinthians 15, where Paul teaches about resurrection, and Revelation 20:12, where all are judged.

Book of Mormon: The Book of Mormon teaches that through Christ's Resurrection, all will be resurrected (Alma 11:42-44), and each will be judged according to their works (Moroni 10:34).

Doctrine and Covenants: In D&C 76, the vision of the degrees of glory (Celestial, Terrestrial, and Telestial kingdoms) is revealed, outlining the final judgment and eternal reward based on one's choices and acceptance of the gospel.

VII. Kingdoms of Glory

Holy Bible: The Bible mentions various degrees of glory (Matthew 5:31-46) and also mentioned in 1 Corinthians 15:40-42.

Book of Mormon: The Book of Mormon reinforces the idea of different rewards after judgment (Alma 40:11-14).

Doctrine and Covenants: D&C 76 offers an expanded vision of the three degrees of glory, teaching that those who accept the gospel will receive varying degrees of glory based on their choices and obedience to Christ's teachings.

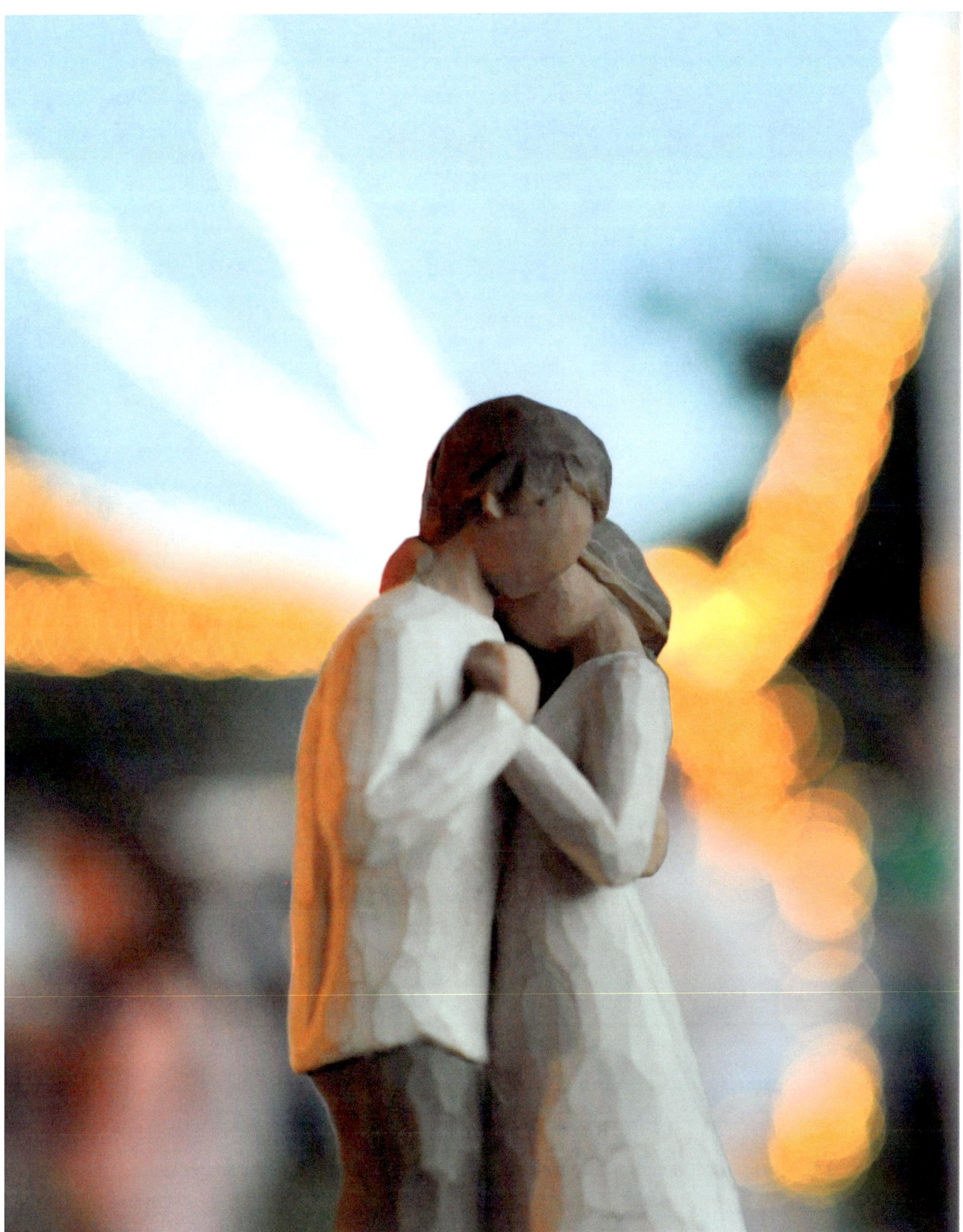

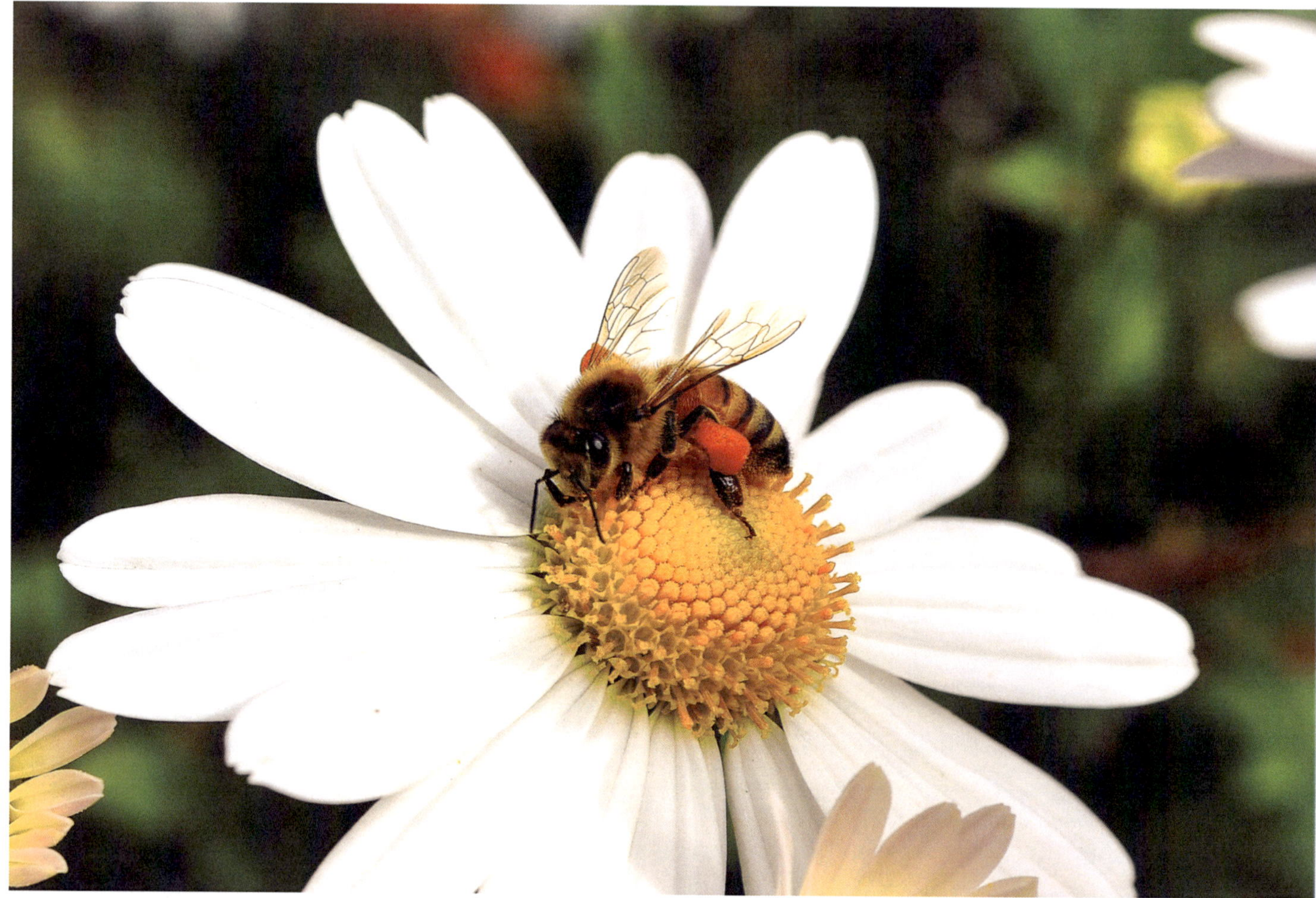

The Holy Bible – *Covers ancient history from the time of Adam and Eve through the life, death, and resurrection of Jesus Christ.*

The Book of Mormon – *Includes the record of the Jaredites, beginning around the time of the Tower of Babel in Genesis, and other writings spanning from approximately 600 B.C. to A.D. 421.*

The Pearl of Great Price – *Contains inspired translations by Joseph Smith of biblical texts, including writings from the time of Moses and Abraham.*

The Doctrine and Covenants – *A compilation of revelations given to modern-day prophets, primarily between 1823 and 1978.*

General Conference Talks and Sacred Writings – *Inspired messages delivered by prophets, apostles, and other church leaders from 1830 to the present day.*

All of these references - and more - demonstrate that God is the same yesterday, today and tomorrow. (Hebrews 13:8, 2 Nephi 27:23)